GEORGE H.W. BUSH

An American Journey

HOUSTON ★ CHRONICLE

Credits

John C. McKeon – Publisher and President

Nancy C. Barnes – Editor and Executive Vice President for News

Mike Tolson – George H.W. Bush: An American Journey writer

Laura E. Goldberg – Project Manager/Senior Editor New & Niche Products

Tony Freemantle – George H.W. Bush: An American Journey Editor/Senior Editor

Scott Kingsley – Director of Multimedia

Susan Barber – Design Director

Charlie Crixell – News Editor

Linda A. Schaible – Vice President of Marketing and Audience Development

Photos from the George Bush Presidential Library and Museum, Houston Chronicle, Houston Post and other Hearst Newspapers archives. Special thanks to **Mary Finch**, Audiovisual Archivist, George Bush Presidential Library and Museum.

Cover Photos – Front: Official portrait of President Bush, 1992. Back: Bush in the Oval Office on the last day of his presidency, Jan. 20, 1993. Both cover photos courtesy David Valdez / The White House and George Bush Presidential Library and Museum

Published by Pediment Publishing, a division of The Pediment Group, Inc. www.pediment.com.
Printed in the United States of America.

George Bush campaigning in Lubbock during his race for the United States Senate, Aug. 29, 1970. *George Bush Presidential Library and Museum*

Contents

JAMES BAKER

BY JAMES A. BAKER III

There has always been something uniquely heroic about George Herbert Walker Bush.

His record, of course, speaks for itself. It tells the story of a rare individual, one who charted a life's course of uncommon achievements that might cower a more ordinary man.

During World War II, he became the youngest naval aviator to date and flew 58 combat missions. His plane was shot down during a successful bombing mission. He won the Distinguished Flying Cross and three Air Medals.

Born in the lap of luxury along America's well-heeled East Coast, he took his family to the hostile environs of the Texas panhandle in search of fortune.

Later, as a politician, he established a track record of backing the "right causes," even if that meant losing political support -- as happened when he supported fair housing legislation as a conservative congressman from Texas whose constituents opposed it.

Throughout the ages, of course, scores of men and women have performed valiantly during times of urgency. Courage, fortitude and bravery are their hallmarks. Medals are testament to their mettle. Certainly, President Bush is among them.

But there is, I believe, an even greater glory to President Bush's brand of heroism, one that is reserved for only the most very special among us.

Quite simply, President Bush dared to be a decent human being. He always had the courage to pursue the traits that every parent hopes for their children -- sincerity, humility, and courtesy. Charity. There was no sham, pretense, apple-polishing or arrogance. What you saw in President Bush is what you got, someone who lived by the Golden Rule.

His mother, Dorothy Bush, played a big role in the development of her son into a decent man. At least, that's what he always said. "Give the other guy credit," he recalls her telling him. "Nobody likes a braggadocio, George. Don't talk about yourself all the time."

Humility remained a core value throughout his life. He rarely talked about his war exploits. In fact, I don't remember him ever doing that. And he didn't write a true memoir following his four years as president, making him the first ex-president not to do so since Woodrow Wilson.

Instead, he said, let the history books tell my story.

Fortunately, those who write history are beginning to understand that he was a great president -- certainly the best one-term president in U.S. history and in my view, one of the greatest of all time.

His record in foreign affairs is simply remarkable. Because of his adroit handling of the Soviet Union, the Cold War ended with a whimper rather than a nuclear bang within a very narrow window of opportunity. Germany was reunited as a member state of NATO. Nuclear arms reduction treaties were signed. America obtained world support to remove Saddam Hussein's troops from Kuwait, won the battle and then had other countries pay for it.

The world was transformed under his calm and studied guidance as president.

Since then, so too has our political culture changed, although not for the better. In recent years, it has grown ugly. Our lack of political comity is appalling to many of us who know how things worked decades ago, when compromise was not a dirty word.

But even sadder is the knowledge that our entire culture is becoming more crass. Vulgarity in speech and thought is becoming a sickening norm. Americans, too often it seems, would rather yell across the divide than listen to one another as a way to strike common ground. Anger and hatred too often have replaced accommodation and compromise.

That's not the way President Bush operated. Using his mother's advice as his guiding light, he listened to his opponents and took counsel from their positions. He was decent to those on both sides of the political aisle. He sought to never lose a friend because of political differences.

In our rush to mythicize our presidents, and too often to demonize them, we should recognize that even without all of his accomplishments, President Bush is, at his very core, a genuinely beautiful human being.

And that may be one of the greatest aspects of his legacy.

Baker was secretary of state and White House chief of staff for President George H.W. Bush

Photos: Godofredo Vasquez / Houston Chronicle

GEORGE H.W. BUSH

Introduction

As his full name might suggest, George Herbert Walker Bush came from a family that had deep roots in America's upper crust. His childhood years in New England were spent in comfort, amid wealth great enough to insulate him from the shocks of the Great Depression and to educate him in the best schools alongside the other old-money offspring. Upon completing his studies at Yale University, alma mater of so many of his forebears, he was expected to take his place in the boardrooms and corner offices of Wall Street, home to the family investment banking business. A continuing path to prosperity, success and perhaps high stature awaited.

And so it might have been in another era, had the world not fallen into chaos. World War II changed everything, pushing millions of boys — rich and poor — prematurely into manhood. This child of privilege soon found himself living in a military melting pot, taking orders from and making friends with people he otherwise would not have met. In short order, he learned what danger and sacrifice really meant, and he saw the cruel democracy of death in the very plane he flew. When the war finally ended, he had a sense that a different era was in the offing.

In 1948, "Poppy" Bush, as his friends universally tagged him, stood ready to graduate from Yale University and take his place in a rearranged social order. Serious and slightly restless, he was certain of only one thing — not wanting a future that looked too much like his past. With millions of ex-soldiers competing for a rung on the career ladder, there may have been good reason for Bush to stay put, to take the Wall Street job. Yet he pushed it away.

The notion of a less predictable future gnawed at him. Bush the soldier had met the challenge before him, performing with grace under pressure, but he was well aware that luck also had played a role. He'd been given a chance denied some of those with whom he had served, and he was determined to somehow prove himself worthy of his good fortune.

OPPOSITE: **Bush photographed at Walker's Point, Kennebunkport, Maine, Aug. 10, 1991.**
George Bush Presidential Library and Museum

Bush had no clear path before him, only a conviction that it would not be easy street. The old and moneyed northeast, with its long-standing network of friends and its clubby familiarity, no longer felt right. Whom his family knew, how much money they had, where he went to college — such things should not define him, he had come to believe.

Of course, that did not mean he was above taking advice or using family contacts. One longtime family friend told Bush to go to Texas and learn the oil business, starting at the bottom. It was a strange but intoxicating notion. As he wrote in a letter to a buddy, the oil patch promised to be "new and exciting." He would be learning something "of basic importance." And he could get rich. There were no guarantees, needless to say, but total failure was an unlikely option if he worked hard. The family friend owned the company.

Off Bush went in a new Studebaker coupe, thus beginning a remarkable journey that would lead him from the elegant estates of New England to the dusty oil fields of the Permian Basin, and later to the leafy precincts of Houston's nicest neighborhoods, to foreign capitals and back to America's own, into political campaigns at the humblest level to one that ultimately netted him the White House — and a final contest that sent him packing again to unwelcome early retirement.

Back in Houston, his adopted hometown, Bush was forced to reinvent himself one last time. No longer a standard bearer, he became the father of one, as well as a not-so-elder statesman who seemed to gain respect by the day and possess the wisdom that was seen as lacking in some of the younger members of his Republican Party. As he moved into his 80s and then past 90, still active and ready to lend his name to a good cause, Bush gained perhaps the ultimate status for a retired president: a place above politics.

Bush's decision to turn away from his family's lucrative financial business turned out to be the right one. His long life has encompassed the full arc of the 20th century and a good chunk of the next one, beginning in an era of steamships and a new ideology called communism and approaching its end as American spaceships explore distant planets and the hammer-and-sickle is mostly a fading emblem on a few old flags. He was the last president of his generation, which came of age during the Great Depression, participated in a cataclysmic world war, and ushered in unprecedented American power and prosperity.

Over the years, there were more electoral defeats than victories, along with personal tragedies that wounded him deeply and haunted him into his later years. There were moments of triumph, broad praise and popularity, and times of great criticism and general confusion about a man who could seem distant and disengaged. When he left the political stage for good, it was hard to know what to make of his roller-coaster career.

As it turned out, the verdict of hindsight has proved more generous than that of a fickle electorate that denied his presidency a second term. Historians universally praise his deft touch in dealing with

LEFT: **173 Adams Street, Milton, Mass., the birthplace of George Herbert Walker Bush. Date unknown.**
George Bush Presidential Library and Museum

diplomatic challenges in Europe and Asia at a crucial time in the evolution of both. And even if his domestic agenda may have suffered by comparison, he scored several legislative achievements and showed a willingness to make tough decisions that were not in his political self-interest.

"I think over the years he fares well," said presidential historian Henry Brands, the author of seven presidential biographies and a professor at the University of Texas. "If voters have a referendum and they vote you down, that automatically puts you down a rung. It's unfair. Bush always was rated very highly by historians more than he was by the public."

Bush occupied the White House from 1988 to 1992, an eventful time that saw the collapse of the Soviet Union, the end of the Berlin Wall and Cold War, a reconfiguration of Europe, the forced removal of Panamanian dictator Manuel Noriega, a nuclear weapons reduction treaty, and the Iraqi invasion of Kuwait, after which he coordinated a 30-nation military response. He gained passage of a North American trade measure that would change the flow of goods, and jobs, in the world's leading economy.

Bush's domestic achievements, rarely getting equal attention, included passage of the signature American with Disabilities Act, a strengthened Clean Air Act, an increased minimum wage, and resolution of the savings-and-loan fiasco. Perhaps most important, he agreed to a deficit-reducing budget deal with Congress that cost him dearly in a political sense but paved the way for a healthy and prosperous period under the leadership of the man who denied his reelection bid, Bill Clinton.

"That set the U.S. on a course for bringing the deficit under control," Brands said. "Clinton owes a lot of the prosperity of the 1990s to Bush."

OPPOSITE: Bush standing in front of a "Yale Fence" in his baseball uniform. Yale University, 1945 to 1948.
George Bush Presidential Library and Museum

LEFT: George Bush, Navy Pilot, 1942 to 1945.
George Bush Presidential Library and Museum

Of Bush it was often said that no one had been better prepared for the presidency. His election capped a career that included two terms in Congress, ambassadorial posts to the United Nations and China (before it was a formal position), leadership of the CIA and eight years as vice president. His public service was no accident. He had expressed interest as a boy, imagining even then some inchoate future greatness, and as an adult watched his father, Prescott, elected to the U.S. Senate. High office was the possible dream.

And Bush treated it as an honorable profession. His turn completed, it was telling that Bush's many years in government yielded few enemies and a legion of officials — elected and otherwise — who spoke of his personal warmth, kindness and essential decency. Political antagonism remained in the political world, rarely seeping into the personal.

"President Bush was inclined to forgive and forget past slights, defeats and even outrages," said longtime aide Chase Untermeyer. "Thus did he offer rides to Maine for Senator George Mitchell, make the daughter of Senator Sam Nunn the head of the Points of Light Foundation, and — to clinch the case — become buddies with Bill Clinton."

From his early days in politics until his final ones, Bush felt strongly about many things. Yet the public — and the voters — too often never saw it, seeing instead a man slightly aloof and void of passion. He disliked appeals that were emotional and eschewed any loss of self-control. Campaigning was a chore because he had been brought up to refrain from boasting or self-promotion. It was unseemly. To many, he was a hazy character. What, really, did he believe in? What was his label?

ABOVE: Bush with an oil field worker, West Texas. Date unknown. *George Bush Presidential Library and Museum*

RIGHT: Bush's daughter Dorothy, 4, shows her support for her father as a Republican candidate for the U.S. Senate at a rally near Richmond, Tx., in 1970.

Dell Van Dusen / Houston Post

The answer is no secret, resting plainly in his distant past. George Bush was a product of his class, his times and his mother's relentless campaign against what she called the "Great I Am." He neither needed nor wanted public adoration, devoting himself instead to a simple principle: good stewardship. Like most born leaders, he just wanted the job.

ABOVE: **George and Barbara Bush in China during his stint as U.S. Envoy to China, 1974-1975.** *George Bush Presidential Library and Museum*

ABOVE MIDDLE: **George and Barbara Bush celebrate his election to Congress, Nov. 1966.** *George Bush Presidential Library and Museum*

ABOVE LEFT: **U.S. Senate candidate George Bush with his father, former U.S. Sen. Prescott Bush, realize it's bad news on election night, Nov. 1964. Bush lost to Democrat Ralph Yarborough.** *Jim Cox / Houston Post*

ABOVE: Bush, as U.S. Ambassador to the United Nations, addresses the General Assembly, circa 1971-1973. *George Bush Presidential Library and Museum*

OPPOSITE: Congressman Bush interviews children using a tape recorder during a fact-finding tour of Vietnam, Dec. 1967- Jan. 1968. *George Bush Presidential Library and Museum*

RIGHT: Republican National Committee Chairman George Bush enjoys boating with his daughter, Doro, and son, Neil, off the coast of Kennebunkport, Maine, Summer 1974. *George Bush Presidential Library and Museum*

BELOW RIGHT: George Bush chats with his mother, Dorothy Walker Bush, at the 1980 Republican National Convention in Detroit shortly after he was named as Ronald Regan's vice presidential running mate. *Sam C. Pierson Jr. / Houston Chronicle*

BELOW: Republican presidential nominee Ronald Reagan and vice presidential nominee George Bush, with their wives Nancy and Barbara, at Houston's Galleria shortly after the 1980 Republican National Convention. *Curtis McGee / Houston Chronicle*

TOP: Vice President George Bush visits the Berlin Wall with German Chancellor Helmut Kohl and Richard von Weizsaecker, Mayor of Berlin, Feb. 1, 1983.
George Bush Presidential Library and Museum

ABOVE: Vice President George Bush fishing in the mountains outside Jackson Hole, Wyo., June, 1987. *George Bush Presidential Library and Museum*

LEFT: Vice President George Bush throws out the first pitch at the All-Star game at the Astrodome in Houston, July, 1986. Barbara Bush is seated at right.
Howard Castleberry / Houston Chronicle

RIGHT: Vice President Bush meets with his and President Ronald Reagan's staff in his office after the March 30, 1981 assassination attempt on Reagan. The group includes Ed Meese, James Baker, Caspar Weinberger, Larry Speakes and Craig Fuller.
George Bush Presidential Library and Museum

BELOW RIGHT: Vice President Bush, President Ronald Reagan, and Soviet Union President Mikhail Gorbachev meet in New York City, December 1988.
George Bush Presidential Library and Museum

BELOW: The note that outgoing President Ronald Reagan left in the Oval Office desk for his successor, President George Bush, on the day of his inauguration, Jan. 20, 1989. *George Bush Presidential Library and Museum*

LEFT: George Bush campaigns for the office of President of the United States, circa 1979.
George Bush Presidential Library and Museum

BELOW LEFT: President George Bush, Arkansas Gov. Bill Clinton, and businessman H. Ross Perot engage in the second Presidential Debate in Richmond, Va., during the 1992 presidential campaign.
George Bush Presidential Library and Museum

BELOW: George and Barbara Bush watch returns on election night in Houston Nov. 8, 1988.
George Bush Presidential Library and Museum

OPPOSITE: President Bush and Barbara Bush greet troops and have Thanksgiving Day dinner at the 1st Marine Division Command Post, Saudi Arabia, Nov. 22, 1990. *George Bush Presidential Library and Museum*

ABOVE: President Bush is met by his grandchildren upon his arrival at Walker's Point in Kennebunkport, Maine, Aug. 15, 1990. *George Bush Presidential Library and Museum*

ABOVE LEFT: President Bush plays in the snow with his grandchildren at Camp David, Jan. 13, 1991. *George Bush Presidential Library and Museum*

LEFT: President Bush demonstrates his horseshoe pitching skills at the White House after Queen Elizabeth of Great Britain presented him with four silver horseshoes engraved with the royal cypher "EIIR," May 14, 1991. *George Bush Presidential Library and Museum*

RIGHT: President Bush and his grandson, Sam LeBlond, take a nap on Air Force One, Feb. 18, 1991.
George Bush Presidential Library and Museum

BELOW RIGHT: President and Mrs. Bush show off the fish he caught in the waters off Walker's Point, Kennebunkport, Maine, Aug. 15, 1990.
George Bush Presidential Library and Museum

BELOW: President Bush on his boat, "Fidelity," catches up on some reading and fishing off the coast of Kennebunkport, Maine, Aug. 16, 1990.
George Bush Presidential Library and Museum

ABOVE: President Bush and Britain's Prince Philip review the Scots Guards in the courtyard of Buckingham Palace, London, June 1, 1989. *George Bush Presidential Library and Museum*

LEFT: President Bush takes his grandson, Sam LeBlond, for a ride on the grounds of Walker's Point, Kennebunkport, Maine, June 2, 1989. *George Bush Presidential Library and Museum*

OPPOSITE: World leaders walk to lunch at Cohen House on the campus of Rice University in Houston after a morning session of the G7 Economic Summit, July 10, 1990. From left to right: Jacques Delors, President of the European Commission; Giulio Andreotti, Prime Minister of Italy; Toshiki Kaifu, Prime Minister of Japan; Margaret Thatcher, Prime Minister of the United Kingdom; François Mitterand, President of France; Helmut Kohl, Chancellor of West Germany; U.S. President George Bush; Brian Mulroney, Prime Minister of Canada. *Nuri Vallbona / Houston Post*

ABOVE: President Bush in the Oval Office on his last day in office, Jan. 20, 1993. *David Valdez / The White House and George Bush Presidential Library and Museum*

ABOVE: President and Mrs. Bush attend the Black Tie and Boots inaugural ball at the Washington Hilton to celebrate being sworn in as the 41st President of the United States, Jan. 21, 1989. *George Bush Presidential Library and Museum*

ABOVE RIGHT: Former President George Bush raises his arms in gratitude as he is welcomed home by neighbors and fans in front of his temporary home in Tanglewood, Houston, Jan. 20 1993. *Kerwin Plevka / Houston Chronicle*

RIGHT: Bush family Christmas photo at Walker's Point, Kennebunkport, Maine, 2000. *George Bush Presidential Library and Museum*

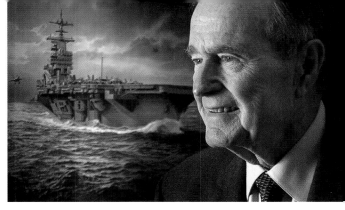

ABOVE: Bush poses for a portrait in his Houston office. Behind him is a rendering of the USS George H.W. Bush, the U.S. Navy aircraft carrier named for him. *Smiley N. Pool / Houston Chronicle*

LEFT: Former U.S. presidents Bush and Bill Clinton walk through debris at Bermuda Beach on Galveston Island in October 2008, inspecting some of the damage inflicted by Hurricane Ike, which had scored a direct hit a month earlier. *Smiley N. Pool / Houston Chronicle*

BELOW: Ever the devoted football fans, George and Barbara Bush on the field during the pregame ceremonies for Super Bowl LI at NRG Stadium in February 2017. *Karen Warren / Houston Chronicle*

Chapter One

From Poppy to George

Bush was born in Milton, Mass., on June 12, 1924, to Prescott and Dorothy Bush, the second of five children, four of them boys. His was an idyllic childhood spent among the nation's economically privileged, with numerous trips to family estates in Maine and South Carolina. Although the hardships of the Great Depression did not severely affect the Bushes, his parents tried to stress that good fortune should not be taken for granted, insisting on modesty at all times along with concern for those going through hard times. Work mattered. Life, they insisted, was no country club affair.

Named for his maternal grandfather, Bush was known as Poppy from his earliest days. The origins of the nickname are not entirely clear — something to do with his dad being "Pop" and him being "Little Pop" — but when he headed off to Greenwich Country Day School for first grade, the nickname went with him. Nobody called him George.

For the next dozen years, Poppy Bush would navigate a world unlike that familiar to most American schoolchildren, first on the manicured lawns of Greenwich and later as a student at Phillips Academy, a famous boarding school in Andover, Mass. He excelled at both schools, performing far above average academically and athletically. He was a favorite of his classmates and often chosen to captain the teams he was on. He had another nickname, "Have Half," because of his habit of sharing whatever treats he had with friends. He was known to call out bullies and protect vulnerable students from them.

As he grew into adolescence, he slowly soaked up the history of generations of Walkers and Bushes and began to understand there were expectations to meet for those of his class and background — a demand to treat others decently and for service to the public good largely divorced from personal gain. Some called it noblesse oblige. He saw it as the natural order of things, and of all the Bush children, young Poppy felt the pull the most deeply.

OPPOSITE: **George Bush (second from right, front row) with his baseball team at Phillips Academy, Andover, Mass., circa 1938.**
George Bush Presidential Library and Museum

ABOVE: Bush at Kennebunkport, Maine, circa 1925, not long after his taking first steps.
George Bush Presidential Library and Museum

RIGHT: Bush's parents, Prescott and Dorothy Walker Bush, with their family. Two future presidents are included, one standing to the left and the other on Dorothy's lap.
George Bush Presidential Library and Museum

"Bush was a figure of an older, fading order of American power," wrote Bush biographer Jon Meacham in "Dynasty and Power", a 2015 authorized biography. "He had come from the world of childhood comfort, prep school noblesse oblige, heroism under fire, and Ivy League polish. When his family and … friends looked at him, they saw a man who could have spent his life making and spending money, but who had chosen to obey the biblical injunction, drilled into him by his parents, that to whom much is given much is expected."

Competition was the way that the natural order winnowed the worthy from the pretenders, and that was fine with Bush, whose amiable nature masked a fierce need to prove himself. He expected to win, and after that to lead with distinction. He spoke with disdain at the notion of something handed to him because of his father's connections or a girl he danced with at a country club party, and he fought such suggestions his entire public life. He recognized the advantages he had from birth, but much of his life amounted to proving he could achieve without them.

LEFT: Prescott and Dorothy Walker Bush, parents of the future president, celebrate Prescott's election to the U.S. Senate. Prescott Bush belonged to the more moderate wing of the Republican Party, reflecting an era in which each of the major political parties contained representatives from across the ideological spectrum. Many of his beliefs were reflected in those of his son, who often was criticized by the party's right wing as too liberal to be a "true" Republican. The two factions would square off in the 1980 presidential election won by Ronald Reagan. *George Bush Presidential Library and Museum*

ABOVE: Bush at summer camp in 1939, only months before the world was plunged into war. *George Bush Presidential Library and Museum*

ABOVE RIGHT: Bush at first base for his Phillips Academy team. The lanky lefthander was a popular student at the famous prep school in Andover, Mass. *George Bush Presidential Library and Museum*

Bush's first great test came as his days at Andover were ending, graduating in the face of a world succumbing to a widening war. He might have been able to use connections for a service academy appointment or a plum job that did not place him in harm's way. Like many of his friends and others of his class, including Joseph and John Kennedy, he chose the opposite path.

Embracing risk was a defining Bush trait, encouraged by Bush's mother from his earliest days. All of her children were expected to climb the towering trees around their home. Neighbors sometimes looked on with shock as the Bush boys made their way from one limb to another. Falls would happen, and sometimes injuries, but the boys grew tougher and more confident. When war came, he was eager to get to it. Military life was the next challenge to be met, which meant the normal next step of his life, the Ivy League degree, would have to wait.

Bush enlisted in the U.S. Navy immediately upon finishing high school in 1942 and hoped to become a pilot. The training went well. As at school, Bush proved adept at learning and making new friends. The military brought his first significant exposure to young men from all walks and classes of American life, but he fit in nonetheless. The outgoing Poppy was a hit. He earned his wings and was commissioned an ensign before his 19th birthday. His wartime duty was spent in the Pacific flying a three-man Avenger torpedo bomber.

Bush piloted 58 combat missions from the carrier USS San Jacinto, but one stood out. During a Sept. 2, 1944, attack on Japanese positions on Chichi-Jima, one of the Bonin Islands, his Avenger was badly hit by flak. He was able to complete the bombing run but had to bail out quickly after finishing it. He ordered the other two crewmen to "hit the silk" as the plane headed toward the water, then he did likewise. He was able to haul himself into a life raft after popping up from the sea, dazed and out of breath. The others were never found.

As he drifted on the current ever closer to the island he had just bombed, Bush suddenly saw a submarine rise from the water. He thought he was delirious, not realizing the USS Finback was on "lifeguard duty" to pick up downed pilots. It was not long before he was laughing and joking with the sub crew, but the death of his crewmates ate away at him, in the

LEFT: After his airplane was shot down, Bush is rescued by crew members of the USS Finback, which was patrolling the waters near the Pacific island of Chichi-Jima to pick up downed flyers, Bush later recalled that he could not believe his eyes when the sub popped up near him, saving him from capture by the Japanese.
George Bush Presidential Library and Museum

RIGHT: A portrait of the pilot as a young man – at the time the youngest participant in the US Navy Primary Flight Training program in Minnesota. Bush joined the Navy in hopes of becoming a flyer as soon as he finished high school.

George Bush Presidential Library and Museum

OPPOSITE: Bush was acknowledged by his peers as one of the best pilots on the USS San Jacinto. Here he smiles from the cockpit of his TBM Avenger torpedo bomber, named for a young woman who would eventually be his wife.

George Bush Presidential Library and Museum

RIGHT: Bush with his two fellow crew members in November 1944: radioman Joe Reichert (left) and turret gunner Leo W. Nadeau. His previous crew perished when their plane was shot down earlier in the year. *George Bush Presidential Library and Museum*

OPPOSITE: Bush in the cockpit of his Avenger going through his checklist.

George Bush Presidential Library and Museum

weeks to come and at odd moments for the rest of his life. Could he have done better by them? Why had he lived and they not? Countless other soldiers asked the same questions, with no answer ever appearing. Sometimes he would weep over the memories of that day and his lost buddies. At times they pushed their way into his dreams.

Bush was awarded the Distinguished Flying Cross, yet he never considered himself a war hero despite the efforts of later political advertising. "They wrote it up as heroism," Bush said late in his life of the paperwork leading to the decoration, "but it wasn't — it was just doing your job."

In January 1945, while on leave from war duty, Bush wed his prewar fiancée, Barbara Pierce. The two had met at a dance when he was at Phillips and she at a tony boarding school in South Carolina. Her family, like his, came from money, with ancestors among the early New England settlers. A distant relative, Franklin Pierce, was the 14th American president.

After the wedding and a quick honeymoon, the couple soberly anticipated the coming months. Bush soon would head back to the Pacific to begin preparations for the invasion of mainland Japan. In the meantime, he was assigned to a base in Michigan for additional training. Both knew that the anticipated loss of life was huge, as the Japanese military government seemed defiantly set on a

RIGHT: Barbara and George on their wedding day, Jan. 6, 1945. They would soon head to a Naval base in Michigan where he would train pilots for the anticipated invasion of Japan. *George Bush Presidential Library and Museum*

OPPOSITE: George and Barbara Bush, the young couple, with his happy and proud parents, Prescott and Dorothy Bush, at their wedding. *George Bush Presidential Library and Museum*

ABOVE: **Eager to get on with his life after his war service, Bush completed his degree in economics at Yale University in two-and-a-half years, but still made time to serve as captain of the school's baseball team. Circa 1948.** *George Bush Presidential Library and Museum*

suicidal last stand. For soldiers in the Pacific, or heading there, it was a gloomy and depressing prospect.

And then, in an instant, all such concerns became moot: Two atomic bombs were dropped on August 6 and 9, leading to Japan's unexpected surrender. A war that had commanded everyone's attention for years, claiming some of his friends and forcing him to mature beyond his years, vanished overnight. It was hard to believe.

Poppy Bush suddenly had a different sort of future to think about. Barbara had dropped out of Smith College, largest of the famed Seven Sisters schools, and accompanied her new husband to his last naval posting. From there it was on to New Haven, Conn., where he would begin his college education at Yale, the alma mater of his father and four other relatives.

He graduated in under three years because of an accelerated program offered to veterans, who were eager to make up for lost time. As at prep school, he excelled at sports and captained the Yale baseball team, for which he played first base as a gangly lefty who hit for average, not power. He was just as adept in the classroom, gaining Phi Beta Kappa distinction and an economics degree. Compared to life on an aircraft carrier, the venerable old campus was a refuge.

Yet, as he later acknowledged, what should have been idyllic college years were not. The class of 1948 was a collection of serious men shaped by armed conflict. Like so many of his peers, Bush approached the postwar world with an undefined urgency. He didn't know what he wanted to do, only that he wanted to get on with it.

As graduation approached, Bush balked at the offer to join a prominent investment bank started by his maternal grandfather. He wrote to a friend about his reservations, especially the idea of taking advantage of "the benefits of my social position." Getting ahead in business because he had attended the same parties as his customers when they were younger struck him as wrong, he said. He wanted something new, not a big house in the Connecticut suburbs and a morning commute to Wall Street.

But what? The East had no shortage of business opportunities, especially for families with connections, but the idea that he kept coming back to was oil, which would take him to Texas. The more he thought about it, with its heady mixture of risk and reward, the more it appealed. Oil drilling was as foreign to him as tightrope walking or fashion design, but it was something different and "something of basic importance," as he wrote to a friend. And it held the promise of great wealth — his own wealth. After all, oil had accounted for the Rockefeller fortune. Other men from the East were heading to the state, which explains how Midland, of all places, had a Yale Club for school alums. Bush decided to join them.

In the summer of 1948, he loaded up their new Studebaker, a graduation gift, and pointed it southwest. Barbara and "Georgie," as their firstborn was then called, flew down after he had rented a weathered duplex that would be their first Texas home. Whether he had a future in the oil business was as yet unknowable, but at least he had a job. The family friend had provided an entry-level sales position with a tool company in Odessa, the bottom rung of the ladder. But it should be noted this was no ordinary friend — Neil Mallon was the head of Dresser Industries, a leading oil field equipment company — which meant Bush's prospects for advancement were good.

As Bush learned the basics of the oil and gas business, he and his growing family were forced to move about, including a stint in California. There was nothing glamorous about his training, which involved every aspect of the tool and hardware side, including the most mundane. On one hot afternoon, he and a coworker were given the task of painting a pumpjack — while it was pumping.

Yet it was the other side of the oil business that held Bush's real interest. By 1950, he, Barbara and their two young children had settled in Midland, where he had formed an oil company with a neighbor, John Overbey. Financial

LEFT: George W. Bush sits on his father's shoulders in New Haven, Conn., April, 1947.
George Bush Presidential Library and Museum

backing came from Bush's father and some of his father's friends and business contacts.

With no geologic or engineering background, Bush learned the business from the ground up, "walking fields, talking to people and trying to make deals," Overbey later recalled in an interview. Three years later, he and Overbey joined up with two brothers, Hugh and William Liedtke, to form Zapata Petroleum. An offshore subsidiary was formed a year later.

Zapata raised more money and gambled on an interest in a field in Coke County that some skeptics claimed was played out. One of the brothers, Bill Liedtke, said years later that the young company drilled 130 wells and never had a dry hole. As for politics, there wasn't much time for it, though Bush did later mention his modest role as a Republican precinct worker. In one particular primary, he later recalled, perhaps apocryphally, only three voters showed up: he, his wife and a drunken Democrat who wandered into the wrong polling station.

Bush enjoyed his time in Midland, learning a business, tending to a growing family and making friends who would prove important later. The closeness of the city's business community was evident when the Bush family's life suddenly was interrupted by tragedy. The second of the children, daughter Robin, was diagnosed with leukemia in 1953, before the disease became largely curable.

Friends did what they could to help and donated blood to assist with Robin's treatment. Bush stopped by a Presbyterian church every morning to pray and later said he felt the presence of the building custodian, hovering nearby, with him every time.

His fledgling business career was all but put on hold for more than six months as he, Barbara and Robin made repeated trips to Sloan Kettering Cancer Center in New York. Barbara tried to approach their demanding new circumstances with stoic resolve, to the point of booting visitors out of Robin's hospital room if they cried. Her husband became increasingly emotional and often had to leave the room. Robin died later in 1953.

"I hadn't cried at all when Robin was alive, but after she died I felt I could cry forever," she recalled in a 1988 interview with Texas Monthly. "George had a much harder time when she was sick. He was just killing himself, while I was very strong. That's the way a good marriage works. Had I cried a lot, he wouldn't have. But then things reversed after she died. George seemed to accept it better."

Robin's loss was the second great tragedy of his life. But unlike the first, this was not the result of the vicissitudes of war. The little girl lingered in their home for years, a source of great memories and endless grief. An oil painting took its place on a wall. She remained an almost-tangible presence as her parents

RIGHT: Bush at his home in Midland, early 1950s. *George Bush Presidential Library and Museum*

OPPOSITE TOP: Bush with his four sons, from left: Neil, Jeb, George W., and Marvin, 1970. *George Bush Presidential Library and Museum*

OPPOSITE BOTTOM LEFT: Bush in the tub with his kids, from left: Neil, Doro, Marvin and Jeb. Circa 1963. *George Bush Presidential Library and Museum*

OPPOSITE BOTTOM RIGHT: The Bush family in Midland, circa 1957. From left to right: George W., Bush, Neil, Marvin (being held by Barbara Bush), and Jeb. *George Bush Presidential Library and Museum* *Courtesy Barbara Bush*

tried to move on.

The Bushes lived in Midland for almost a decade. It was where he made his first real money — his own money — and where he established his image as a true, if transplanted, Texan, one who could down a bowl of chili at lunch and a chicken-fried steak at dinner, snacking in between on pork rinds. Everyone in town knew George Bush — Poppy had been jettisoned along with the Brooks Brothers suits — but isolated West Texas was not where he needed to be.

A disagreement over the future direction of the company led Bush to buy out the other investors in Zapata Offshore in 1959. He soon moved the company to Houston. The stakes increased as the company pursued drilling at the bottom of the Gulf of Mexico and the expensive rigs required to do it. If the wells fizzled, the company likely would go under and Bush would end up broke, possibly to head back to New England with his tail between his legs. The stress of potential calamity, a constant for smaller operators, caused endless insomnia and a bad stomach. But fortune smiled. The company ultimately prospered.

Chapter Two

The Call of Politics

During the early 1960s, Bush began to feel the political itch, or, to be more precise, respond to an itch that had been there for years. The family thirst for competition and imperative of public service had been suppressed but never denied. Houston Republicans saw a potential star, a young executive who was smart, good-looking and ambitious. His Eastern pedigree was a double-edged sword — helpful with party elites but a source of suspicion for the ultra-conservative faction — and would remain that way.

Bush had grown up in a Republican Party that was dramatically different than what it came to look like in his later years. It included moderate and liberal factions whose members sometimes disagreed with one another as much as they did with Democrats. Like his father, who had served two terms in the U.S. Senate, the patrician Bush was by nature a pragmatist. He believed his job was to get something done, taking incremental steps when big ones were unobtainable. He had no use for those who would sacrifice progress on the altar of philosophical purity, nor did he regard opponents as enemies.

Bush started electoral politics with a successful race for Harris County GOP chairman. It was a small position, and not actually a government job, but he had been asked to run in order to make sure it did not fall into the hands of perceived extremists in the party's right wing, many of whom were members of the conspiracy-hawking John Birch Society.

OPPOSITE: **Bush speaks at a rally in San Antonio during his first presidential race, May 2, 1980.** *San Antonio Express-News*

LEFT: **Bush campaigning with friend Will Farish during his U.S. Senate race in 1964.** *George Bush Presidential Library and Museum*

RIGHT: U.S. Senate candidate George Bush officially kicks of his statewide campaign at a rally in Houston's Music Hall, Sept. 17, 1964. *Houston Post*

FAR RIGHT: Bush stands next to a campaign poster during his unsuccessful run for a seat in the U.S. Senate, 1964. *George Bush Presidential Library and Museum*

OPPOSITE LEFT: Newly elected Congressman George Bush and family in Washington, DC, 1966. *George Bush Presidential Library and Museum*

OPPOSITE TOP RIGHT: Bush flashes a winner's smile as his wife, Barbara, gives him a victory kiss following his election to a seat in the U.S. Congress from the 7th district in Texas. *Jerry Click / Houston Post*

OPPOSITE BOTTOM RIGHT: George and Barbara on the night he was elected to Congress, 1966. *George Bush Presidential Library and Museum*

Perhaps because his father, Prescott, had just left the U.S. Senate, Bush brashly decided to take on incumbent U.S. Sen. Ralph Yarborough in 1964. Once again, he showed his taste for risk, knowing from the outset that he would be an underdog but believing Yarborough was too liberal for a state like Texas.

Though little known outside of Houston and Midland, Bush campaigned vigorously as a different sort of Republican, less in step with the northeastern wing of his father and closer to the politics of Barry Goldwater and George Wallace. What he was hearing encouraged him. Harris County had been the largest metro area in the country to go for the 1960 Republican ticket of Richard Nixon and Henry Cabot Lodge. Bush sensed the tide was turning against the Democrats in Texas.

He was correct, if premature. Bush went full-tilt conservative, opposing the pending Civil Rights Bill, denouncing the proposed Medicare and food stamps, and arguing the federal government should not be involved in infrastructure projects.

Internationally, he opposed admitting China to the United Nations, supported escalation of the war in Vietnam, and promoted a policy of arming expatriate Cubans to invade the country and overthrow the

Castro government. He also embraced the support of Birch Society members, even if he disagreed with most of what they stood for.

Yarborough portrayed Bush as an extremist and easily defeated him, gaining 56 percent of the vote as Lyndon Johnson swamped Barry Goldwater in the presidential race. Then again, a little-known guy with no track record had claimed 44 percent of the vote in a big year for Democrats. Bush's candidacy showed that a GOP alliance with voters who supported segregation, opposed anti-poverty efforts, and believed in U.S. military domination wherever possible would pull away southern Democrats who were increasingly at odds with the more liberal faction of their party.

After his defeat, Bush struggled to reconcile his moderate views with an election that had seen him embrace, however tentatively, an anti-progressive tone and a segregationist posture. He conceded he was pushed in that direction, and he lamented the increasing prominence of the ultra-conservatives in the party. He would never go so far again.

"This mean, humorless philosophy which says everybody should agree on absolutely everything is not good for the Republican Party or our state," Bush wrote to a friend after the loss. "When the word moderate becomes a dirty word, we have some soul searching to do."

Those sentiments would become increasingly prophetic in coming decades. For now, it was Bush's task to find a significant election he could win. Local government was too limiting for his taste — he had already mentioned a dream of someday becoming president — so he settled on a new congressional seat that ironically had been created following a redistricting lawsuit that he had filed on behalf of the local GOP. Much of the district was in west Houston, the large affluent portions of which made the seat very winnable.

He announced in January 1966 and in November defeated District Attorney Frank Briscoe. He was the first Republican from Houston elected to Congress and the star of the growing Texas GOP. Once in Washington, he ended up with a plum appointment to the Ways and Means Committee — a party nod to the importance of Texas. His voting record was predictably conservative, though not as hard right as his previous rhetoric suggested. He backed away from some of the right-wing stands of

ABOVE: Congressman Bush as he departs Houston on a fact-finding trip to Vietnam in December, 1967 during the war. As a newly elected Congressman, Bush financed the 16-day tour to look at "the other war" in Vietnam, and to determine if the Vietnamese government and people were committed to the war effort. *Dan Hardy / Houston Post*

two years earlier and ended up voting for the Civil Rights Bill, as a result receiving stacks of hate mail and some death threats.

"I want (the party's) conservatism to be sensitive and dynamic, not scared and reactionary," Bush told the Wall Street Journal at the time.

Although new members of Congress typically serve in obscurity, Bush naturally seemed to find his place, and fast. He was invited to the best parties and quickly was taken into the Chowder and Marching Society, an informal club of GOP comers. With Bush's father quietly helping to pave the way for what appeared to be an up-and-comer, he hit the Washington turf running.

There was but one problem — he had no patience for slowly working his way up the House ladder, dutifully toiling away on one subcommittee after another. He also was bored by basic constituent work, assisting with their endless small problems. Though only 42 when elected, he considered himself a big-picture guy, inclined toward matters of national policy and important issues, not a political factory worker.

Bush was in his second term in 1970 when President Nixon mentioned to him that he was eager to knock off Yarborough, a persistent critic. Nixon wanted to know if he was willing to try again.

Bush was more than willing, and his instinct told him that Yarborough's time was at an end. The Texas liberal icon simply did not mesh with the state's increasingly conservative drift.

Bush's timing with respect to Yarborough was spot-on. But a former Texas congressman named Lloyd Bentsen had the same idea. Coming from a prominent family in the Rio Grande Valley, he also had been a bomber pilot during World War II and had moved to Houston to establish a business career after three terms in the House of Representatives. When Bentsen knocked off the liberal incumbent, Bush found himself in a race he had not anticipated, running against a candidate who looked much like himself: smart, centrist, attractive to a new generation.

Bush lost again. It was not a rout, and Bush's 47 percent showing suggested that Democratic dominance might be nearing an end. In other parts of the country, his performance put him in a positive light. But the fact was that Bush, after two terms in Congress, did not have a job. He had given up his business to pursue the one thing he had always wanted. He needed something to do.

ABOVE: After serving two terms in Congress, Bush again mounted a campaign for the U.S. Senate, opening his headquarters in Harris County on April 2, 1970. *Jim Cox / Houston Post*

ABOVE RIGHT: Bush in a decked-out Volkswagen attends a hamburger fry in Marshall during his 1970 campaign for a seat in the U.S. Senate. *George Bush Presidential Library and Museum*

OPPOSITE: Bush, a Republican candidate for the U.S. Senate, speaks at the opening of his Harris County campaign headquarters, April 1970. *Sam C. Pierson Jr. / Houston Chronicle*

Since Nixon had pushed him toward the Senate bid, he responded by appointing Bush to be U.S. ambassador to the United Nations. Nixon had been cool to the appointment, uncertain Bush was right for it. But for the ambitious young hopeful it was a welcome opportunity, giving him an introduction to diplomacy and world affairs while removing him from the daily political grind. Some critics felt he did not have the requisite experience and were wary of his Eastern elite background, but there was no mounted opposition to him. He served in the post from 1971 to 1973.

What followed over the rest of the decade was a series of appointed posts, none precisely what he was wanting but each of which gave him useful experience. First, after Nixon's landslide reelection, came the chairmanship of the Republican National Committee. His tenure coincided with investigations into the Watergate affair, which eventually resulted in Nixon's resignation. Although Bush survived untainted, new President Gerald Ford knew it was time for a change and appointed him "envoy" to China — the two nations did not yet have full diplomatic relations, so Bush could not be called an ambassador.

In Ford's final year in office, another staff shake-up found Bush appointed in 1976 to be director of the Central Intelligence Agency, which was in disarray after years of scandalous revelations. He was there

The Call of Politics • 59

only a year, not long enough to enact major reforms or personnel changes. He was given credit for greatly restoring the agency's morale when it was at its lowest point, and he was well thought of by longtime agency hands. The main building at the agency's headquarters in Langley, Va., was renamed in his honor in 1999.

When Ford was defeated by Jimmy Carter later that year, Bush offered to stay at the CIA. His gesture was turned down and he again found himself unemployed. Returning to Houston, he served on the executive committee of a local bank, taught courses at Rice University and was made director of the Council on Foreign Relations, the prestigious national foreign policy organization. But it wasn't enough.

Getting back into politics never was far from his mind. In truth, he was bored with private life. He felt he was in the prime of his intellectual life, and he lacked a challenge worthy of it.

"I've been tense as a coiled spring," Bush wrote to a friend not long after coming home to Texas. "There is a missing of stimulating talk. I just get bored silly about whose daughter is a Pi Phi .... I don't want to slip into that 3 or 4 martini late lunch rich social thing. There is too much to learn still."

But what to do? Considering his total experience as an elected officeholder was four years — the two terms in Congress — some might have thought of another run at the U.S. Senate, or perhaps governor, high positions that often lead to presidential bids. But Bush, confident of his ability, dreamed of the top job in the land.

The Democrats were in the

ABOVE: The Bush family gathers for a group photo during the 1970 campaign for the U.S. Senate. *George Bush Presidential Library and Museum*

White House and not faring well. In the view of many, Carter's team of self-proclaimed outsiders did not seem up to the demands of national and international leadership. The GOP believed it had a great chance to take it back. George Bush as president? He didn't discount the notion.

Despite the brevity of his time in elected office, Bush was billed as "the president you don't have to train." His knowledge of the Washington power structure and of the demands of geopolitics were immensely greater than his opponents as the various presidential campaigns ramped up ahead of the 1980 elections. But once more, he found himself in the wrong place at the wrong time.

His chief opponent was Ronald Reagan, who was well on his way to becoming a conservative icon.

Gradually, the Republican Party was becoming a party of the right. Bush, whose family had been players in the GOP when Reagan was still an actor and a Democrat, found himself assailed as a liberal along the lines of Nelson Rockefeller, who had been dumped from the 1976 presidential ticket because of his unpopularity. Bush may have presented a nice contrast to Carter, who many believed was out of his depth, but Reagan was the rising power in a party that wanted to prune its more liberal members, and many of the moderates as well.

Bush claimed an early win in Iowa, and as spring wore on he scored big primary wins in some important states. But not enough. With just a few major primaries to go, he had a mathematical chance to claim the nomination if he could win in California. But that was unlikely, to say the least. He did not want to drop out — a Bush was not a quitter — but longtime friend and campaign manager James Baker managed to convince him the numbers would not add up. Bush agreed, reluctantly. He was seen writing on a notepad, "Never give up. Never never." Yet as much as he wanted to convince himself, facts were facts. If he pushed the fight to the bitter end, he would jeopardize any consideration as Reagan's running mate.

Then again, whether he had a political future even as No. 2 was in doubt. That slender lifeline was held by a man who did not hold him in high regard. Reagan was angered by Bush's campaign complaints about his age and his comments about Reagan's economic strategy, the "voodoo economics" line that had already entered the political lexicon. He regarded Bush as heir to the faction of old elites he wanted to push to the sideline. That the GOP still included moderates at all was an annoyance to the gung-ho movement of conservatives who longed for a political and cultural revolution.

Bush dutifully showed up at the 1980 Republican National Convention skeptical that Reagan would offer him the vice presidency. He was determined to exit with grace, at one point scolding son Jeb for

LEFT: George W. Bush, center, joins his mother, Barbara Bush, and brother, Jeb Bush, rear, in Houston as his father acknowledges defeat in the 1970 U.S. Senate race. The younger Bush campaigned vigorously for his father in the race against Democrat Lloyd Bentsen Jr. *Sam C. Pierson Jr. / Houston Chronicle*

FAR LEFT: George and Barbara Bush watch election returns at the Shamrock Hilton Hotel in Houston, Nov. 3, 1970. Bush lost his bid for a U.S. Senate seat to Lloyd Bentsen. *Dan Hardy / Houston Post*

OPPOSITE TOP LEFT: In December, 1970 President Richard Nixon named Bush the U.S. Ambassador to the United Nations. *George Bush Presidential Library and Museum*

OPPOSITE BOTTOM LEFT: Bush, newly minted as the U.S. Ambassador to the United Nations, presents his credentials to Secretary-General U Thant, March 1, 1971. *George Bush Presidential Library and Museum*

OPPOSITE RIGHT: Bush and his wife Barbara pose for a photo during his term as U.S. Ambassador to the United Nations, 1971-1973. *George Bush Presidential Library and Museum*

LEFT: After his stint as Ambassador to the U.N., President Richard Nixon named Bush Chairman of the Republican National Committee. Here he meets with Nixon and others in the Oval Office, May 1973. *George Bush Presidential Library and Museum*

FAR LEFT: Bush and his wife Barbara in China. President Gerald Ford appointed Bush as the U.S. "envoy" to China in 1974. The two nations did not yet have full diplomatic relations, so Bush could not be called an ambassador. *George Bush Presidential Library and Museum*

having complained about the unfairness of having lost to a candidate he considered less qualified.

"What are you talking about, fair!" Bush snapped, according to family recollections. "This is politics. Nobody owes us a damn thing."

Jeb got the blunt family reminder: A Bush did not whine about losing. Contests were to be won, certainly, but Reagan had claimed more delegates and his father was determined to go out with dignity intact, chin up and head high. Though Bush still had a large and loyal following, Reagan was clear about not wanting him as his vice president.

Yet, as the convention dragged on, there was no other obvious choice for running mate. There were lengthy discussions with Ford that ultimately went nowhere. GOP tacticians were afraid of pairing Reagan with another hard-core right candidate who might make the ticket seem too extremist. Even if Reagan didn't prefer Bush, business was business.

Just before midnight, as the convention's final day loomed, common sense trumped Reagan's personal feelings. Baker picked up the phone in Bush's hotel suite, then handed the receiver to the failed candidate. Bush had his reprieve. The vice presidency was less than ideal, but preferable to the alternative.

"Out of a clear blue sky, the phone rang," Bush later recalled for his biographer Meacham. "I thought we were done, out of it, just gone."

Over the next eight years, the relationship between the two men grew increasingly warm and cordial. Bush would prove a loyal second to Reagan, never pursuing his own agenda or separating himself from White House policy. To the contrary, he was relied on to carry out key assignments.

There was little doubt after Reagan's reelection in 1984 that Bush would follow with another campaign

ABOVE: A formal portrait of Bush in his office as Republican National Committee Chairman, 1973-1974.
George Bush Presidential Library and Museum

ABOVE MIDDLE: Bush visits the Great Wall of China during his service as U.S. envoy to the communist country in 1975.
George Bush Presidential Library and Museum

ABOVE RIGHT: Bush, U.S. Secretary of State Henry Kissinger and Chairman Deng Xiaoping at a meeting in Beijing, Nov. 1974.
George Bush Presidential Library and Museum

of his own. Planning and preparations began early. With no incumbent, the field would be larger. Yet no major figure emerged. Bush's biggest challenger turned out to be Kansas Sen. Bob Dole, whose campaign fizzled early.

From the first day of his campaign — literally — Bush made it clear that he was not attempting to step into Reagan's shoes.

"I do not yearn to lead a crusade," Bush said in his formal announcement. "I have held high office and done the work of democracy day by day. I am a practical man. I like what's real. I'm not much for the airy and abstract. I like what works."

As the GOP moved toward a defiant brand of ultra-conservatism, Bush and his Ivy League background, as well as his strong roots in the establishment, moderate middle of the party, had become a tougher sell. Most of the new movement conservatives who had backed Reagan never trusted or believed in him. Then again, they had no strong candidate of their own. And he was by any measure preferable to the candidate who emerged from the Democratic primaries: Massachusetts Gov. Michael Dukakis.

The campaign for the presidency came down to a simple question: Was Dukakis too liberal for a majority of the electorate? Bush knew the question well, for he had faced it in various campaigns for Republican office. He had to walk a fine line, appealing to the moderate mass of independent voters while not alienating the Reagan supporters.

Even if most of Bush's political experience came via appointed positions, the battle of the résumés clearly gave him the nod. All he had to do was sell it. His acceptance speech at the 1988 Republican convention focused on who he was, not the great visionary he wasn't: capable and compassionate, progressive to a point and pragmatic to a fault, decent but determined.

Bush hoped to push aside the notion that he was an aloof patrician who had little understanding of the world inhabited by the less fortunate. He used the words of speechwriter Peggy Noonan to describe the sort of conservatism that he believed in, which was at odds with the hawkish, devil-take-the-hindmost philosophy of some in the party's right wing.

"Prosperity with a purpose means taking your idealism and making it concrete by certain acts of goodness," Bush said. "It means helping a child from an unhappy home learn how to read — and I thank my wife Barbara for all her work in literacy. It means teaching troubled children through your presence that there's such a thing as reliable love. Some would say it's soft and insufficiently tough to care about these things. But where is it written that we must act as if we do not care, as if we are not moved? Well I am moved. I want a kinder, gentler nation."

Bush also wanted people to believe he understood the concerns of middle Americans, which was why he agreed to utter the words that would come back to dog his every day in a later campaign, words at odds with the sort of political leader he was — words he should have been smart enough to avoid at all costs.

LEFT: Bush is sworn in as Director of the CIA by U.S. Supreme Court Justice Potter Stewart as President Gerald Ford looks on, Jan. 30, 1976. *George Bush Presidential Library and Museum*

ABOVE: George and Barbara Bush drink tea with local citizens during their visit to Tibet in 1977. *George Bush Presidential Library and Museum*

OPPOSITE: Bush poses for a portrait at his desk as Director of the Central Intelligence Agency, 1976-1977.

George Bush Presidential Library and Museum

Read my lips: No new taxes.

Some of Bush's advisers urged him to remove the dramatic pledge to reject all tax increases. It was not realistic, given the competing realities of a rising deficit and a Congress controlled by Democrats. Noonan wanted them back in. It sounded emphatic. It sounded dramatic. Of course, Noonan was concerned with rhetorical resonance, not practical politics. Bush finally agreed for a simple reason. He really wanted the job.

OPPOSITE: At the Republican National Convention in 1980, Ronald Reagan, who bested Bush in the contest for the party's presidential nomination, chose Bush as his running mate for the election in November. The candidates and their wives, Nancy Reagan and Barbara Bush, made their first post- convention public appearance at Houston's Galleria shopping mall. *David Breslauer / Houston Chronicle*

ABOVE: Bush returned in triumph to greet his neighbors near his Houston home after being tapped by Ronald Reagan vice presidential running mate, July 19, 1980. *David Breslauer / Houston Chronicle*

OPPOSITE: Bush fires up supporters at a rally in Houston's Sam Houston Park while seeking the Republican Party's nomination for president, May, 1979. *Timothy Bullard / Houston Chronicle*

ABOVE: As the vice presidential nominee, Bush shakes hands with a young player with Mariachi Infantil Guadalupano while stumping in Mission County Park in San Antonio, Sept. 7, 1980. *San Antonio Express-News*

LEFT: In a vice presidential campaign swing across Texas, Bush paused for an interview at the San Antonio International Airport in 1980. *San Antonio Express-News*

OPPOSITE: Bush shakes hands with a supporter at a rally in San Antonio's Mission County Park while campaigning for the Reagan/Bush Republican ticket, Sept. 7, 1980. *San Antonio Express-News*

ABOVE: Bush, the Republican vice presidential nominee, and his presidential campaign manager, James A. Baker III of Houston, go over plans for a victory rally planned for Houston following the Republican National Convention in Detroit. *Sam C. Pierson Jr. / Houston Chronicle*

LEFT: Bush and his wife Barbara celebrate his election as Vice President of the United States at the Houston Oaks Hotel in Houston, Nov. 4, 1980. *Bill Thompson / Houston Post*

ABOVE: Bush holds a press conference in Houston before leaving for Washington, DC to meet with President-elect Ronald Reagan and begin work on the transition, Nov. 10, 1980.

Betty Tichich / Houston Post

LEFT: Bush, flanked by his wife Barbara, is sworn in as Vice President of the United States, Jan. 20, 1981. *George Bush Presidential Library and Museum*

BELOW LEFT: Bush delivers an address at Texas Southern University, May, 1981. *Timothy Bullard / Houston Chronicle*

BELOW RIGHT: Bush and President Ronald Reagan at a Press Club Dinner in Washington, Feb., 1981. *George Bush Presidential Library and Museum*

RIGHT: Bush participates in a teleconference with the crew of Space Shuttle Columbia, April, 1981.
George Bush Presidential Library and Museum

BELOW LEFT AND RIGHT: Bush confers with his staff on board Air Force Two headed back to Washington, DC, after the assassination attempt on President Reagan, March 30, 1981.
George Bush Presidential Library and Museum

OPPOSITE: Bush and Reagan in the Oval Office, Jan. 22, 1982.
George Bush Presidential Library and Museum

ABOVE RIGHT: Vice President Bush participates in a briefing at Hill 229 in the Demilitarized Zone in Korea, April 25, 1982. *George Bush Presidential Library and Museum*

MIDDLE RIGHT: Vice President Bush with Chinese Vice Chairman Deng Xiaoping in China, May 8, 1982. *George Bush Presidential Library and Museum*

BELOW RIGHT: Bush attends the dedication ceremony for the new U.S. Army Reserve training center in Houston, Dec., 1983. The center was named for Macario Garcia, a World War II Congressional Medal of Honor recipient, whose widow, Alice Garcia was also in attendance. *King Chou Wong / Houston Post*

OPPOSITE: Bush speaks at a Houston voter registration drive, dubbed the Reagan Roundup, held at a Houston hotel during the 1984 re-election campaign. *Carlos Antonio Rios / Houston Chronicle*

TOP: Bush delivers the Texas A&M University Commencement Address in College Station, May 1984. *George Bush Presidential Library and Museum*

ABOVE: Bush speaks at a political forum at Texas A&M University in College Station, September 1984. *George Bush Presidential Library and Museum*

RIGHT: Bush meets with Prime Minister Thatcher in London, February 1984. *George Bush Presidential Library and Museum*

LEFT: Bush meets with People's Republic of China Premier Zhao Ziyang in China, Oct., 1985.
George Bush Presidential Library and Museum

FAR LEFT: Bush is sworn in for a second term as Vice President by Supreme Court Justice Potter Stewart during a private swearing-in ceremony at the White House, Jan. 20, 1985.
George Bush Presidential Library and Museum

BELOW LEFT: School teacher Christa McAuliffe speaks following the announcement by Bush that she will be the first private citizen to serve as an astronaut aboard the space shuttle, July, 1985. Six months later, McAuliffe and six fellow astronauts perished when Space Shuttle Challenger exploded shortly after lift-off from its launch pad at the Kennedy Space Center in Florida.
George Bush Presidential Library and Museum

ABOVE: Vice President Bush and his wife Barbara visit a camp for victims of a drought in El Obeid, Sudan, March 1985. *George Bush Presidential Library and Museum*

LEFT: Bush faces photographers as he prepares to throw out the first pitch at the All-Star Game at the Astrodome, July 15, 1986.
Larry Reese / Houston Chronicle

BELOW LEFT: The Bushes participate in the Columbus Day Parade in Chicago, Ill., October 1986.
George Bush Presidential Library and Museum

BELOW RIGHT: A formal portrait of Vice President George Bush, July 23, 1986.
George Bush Presidential Library and Museum

OPPOSITE: Bush officially launched his 1988 presidential campaign in the main ballroom of the Hyatt Regency Hotel in Houston on Oct. 12, 1987. The announcement party moved from the ballroom to the hotel's massive lobby where the elevators were decorated with lights spelling out "Bush 88." *Mary Urech Stallings / Houston Post*

LEFT: Bush and wife Barbara hide behind a sombrero during a Cinco de Mayo event at Hogg Middle School in Houston, May 5, 1987. *John Van Beekum / Houston Chronicle*

BELOW LEFT: Bush dons a cowboy hat. Place unknown. 1988. *Steve Campbell / Houston Chronicle*

ABOVE: Bush, the Republican candidate for president, serves as grand marshal of the Houston Livestock Show and Rodeo parade in downtown Houston, Feb. 20, 1988. *Jerry Click / Houston Post*

ABOVE: Reagan and Bush, accompanied by wives Nancy and Barbara, join hands after the President endorses Bush's candidacy for president during the President's Dinner, Washington, DC, May 11, 1988. *George Bush Presidential Library and Museum*

TOP: Bush delivers his acceptance speech at the Republican National Convention, New Orleans, La., Aug. 18 1988.
George Bush Presidential Library and Museum

ABOVE: The Bush family greets delegates at the Republican National Convention in New Orleans, Aug. 18, 1988.
George Bush Presidential Library and Museum

RIGHT: Bush acknowledges delegates attending the Texas Republican Party Convention at the George R. Brown Convention Center, June 1988. Behind him are his wife, Barbara Bush, and Texas GOP Chairman George Strake Jr.
Craig Hartley / Houston Post

ABOVE: Former President Bush wipes a tear as he, wife Barbara, and son Jeb applaud the inauguration of George W. Bush as governor of Texas in Austin, January 1995.

Kerwin Plevka / Houston Chronicle

Chapter Three

The Oval Office

As the 1988 race took off, Bush was in trouble. He was down in the polls, and even those who figured on voting for him had a hard time getting excited. While Bush was confident, those around him were much less so. Finally, advisers Lee Atwater and Roger Ailes persuaded him to unleash a negative assault on Dukakis, who in short order would become a soft-on-crime pacifist who gave murderers weekend passes, proudly waved his ACLU membership card, opposed the death penalty, and didn't believe in the Pledge of Allegiance.

Bush faced a caricature attack of his own: He was a fuzzy and over-ambitious elitist who believed the presidency was his by right, or perhaps an ex-preppy dilettante more interested in those at the top of the ladder than at the bottom. To critics, he appeared unable or uninterested in articulating any great theme of leadership that would justify making him president.

Bush's advisers successfully pushed a narrow, simple message designed to portray Dukakis as too far to the left of the American people. Ads produced by an outside conservative group told the story of Willie Horton, who had committed a horrible, violent crime while out on one of the weekend passes that had been available to some Massachusetts prisoners. Quickly Horton, who was black, became a household name.

The Bush camp was accused of endorsing a

OPPOSITE: **President-elect George Bush acknowledges the cheers of supporters at his victory celebration at the George R. Brown Convention Center, Nov. 8, 1988. Bush defeated Mass. Gov. Michael Dukakis to retain the White House for the Republican Party.** *Dave Einsel / Houston Chronicle*

LEFT: **San Antonio Mayor Henry Cisneros and Vice President Bush ride a float along Houston Street on March 2, 1986, during a parade marking the 150th anniversary of the Texas Declaration of Independence.** *San Antonio Express-News*

ABOVE: Bush arrives via barge at the Arneson River Theater in San Antonio for a rally during his presidential campaign, Aug. 25, 1988. *San Antonio Express-News*

RIGHT: Bush on the presidential campaign trail in North Augusta, S.C., March 1988. *George Bush Presidential Library and Museum*

commercial that some claimed carried racist overtones because of its use of Horton's mug shot. Eventually his campaign denounced the ad, trying to distance itself from any implicit message. But it did not shy away from the gist of it, a criticism first raised by one of Dukakis' Democratic opponents, Al Gore. The Horton ad resonated, at least in part, because it contained a strong element of truth.

As summer turned to fall, Bush kept rising in the polls. His blend of experience and apparent moderation made for a more compelling image than the admittedly liberal northeastern governor, who remained on the defensive. The election was a decisive victory. Bush carried 40 states and claimed more than 53 percent of the vote.

In his inaugural address, Bush lamented a changing political culture that embraced meanness and hostility — a coarse competition that was anathema to his family's personal code — and he hinted that his style of leadership would be short on grand gestures and bold posturing.

"I see history as a book with many pages, and each day we fill a page with acts of hopefulness and meaning," Bush said.

LEFT: Barbara Bush reaches out to stifle a granddaughter's yawn as her husband delivers his victory speech after being elected President of the United States, Nov. 8, 1988. *Richard Carson / Houston Chronicle*

BELOW: President-elect George Bush, his wife, Barbara, and his grandchildren, Jenna (left) and Barbara wave to well-wishers while boarding Air Force Two at Ellington Field to return to Washington the day after his election victory. *King Chou Wong / Houston Post*

A day that he had long imagined, and which had seemed less likely with each passing defeat, finally arrived. Bush had never boasted the star power needed for a flamboyant political rise. But he had impressed enough people at each step to remain useful in government, and from each setback he had shown a knack for what longtime aide Untermeyer calls "bouncing upwards in life." He was friendly by nature, avoided the traps that led to feuds, and devoted himself to the task at hand. He had loyally served others, especially Reagan.

Now it was his turn. Better prepared than most who take over the Oval Office, Bush was unflinching in his confidence that he could manage the federal government. He envisioned eight years of work that would advance much of Reagan's agenda but temper it with a dose of moderation, where needed, and change the harsh tone imposed by movement conservatives.

Bush was neither awed by the position nor inspired by great acts he hoped to push into law. How others would measure him someday never was a concern. He continually batted away any questions about legacy, even years after he had left office. Such matters were the stuff of vanity.

"He was never a man interested in the past," Untermeyer said. "He was focused on the present and the future."

The presidency was simply the business end of forward-looking governance, and it was his job to make as many good decisions as he could. The use of power, he intoned at his inauguration, was only in service to the people. Untermeyer described him as an "in-box president" who dealt with the matters of the day, worked diligently to resolve them, then moved on.

Bush's diary entries of the time tell of his practical approach to a job that could be overwhelming: "Family, faith, friends, do your best, try your hardest. Rely on the innate good sense, kindness, and understanding of the American people."

Some American presidencies happen to fall at quiet times globally, allowing them to be focused on domestic matters. Bush's term was not one of them. This, of course, was to his good fortune. He was a practiced hand at international relations and had developed personal relationships with a number of key foreign figures.

Bush had not been in the White House long when the Berlin Wall fell in 1989, a principal signal that the Soviet bloc was in its final days and that his administration would soon see its first big test. Displaying considerable judgment and self-control, Bush rejected suggestions of numerous American politicians and pundits and refused to dance on the rubble of the communist empire, lest he complicate the task of Kremlin leaders in managing their crumbling universe or the West German government in moving to reunify the nation at the heart of Europe.

Central to his desire to bolster a new relationship with the crumbling Soviet Union was his personal contact with its reformist leader, Mikhail Gorbachev. The two met formally in 1989 at the Malta Summit, where they discussed the changing geopolitical landscape and announced a formal end to the Cold War.

ABOVE: Bush and Republican consultant Lee Atwater join forces to play the guitar at the Celebration for Young Americans in Washington, DC, in January 1989. Bush was not likely to impress anyone with his musical prowess, but Atwater was an accomplished guitarist who had played professionally.
George Bush Presidential Library and Museum

"We can realize a lasting peace and transform the East-West relationship to one of enduring cooperation," Bush said at the summit's end. True to the history of such predictions, it did not prove accurate, as the steady rise of Vladimir Putin presented a new challenge. But in any case, Bush and Gorbachev met again in Washington in 1990, and their cordial relationship remained long after each left public office.

Bush's cautious posture as the Soviet Union was beginning to unravel was a highlight of his presidency. Understanding that an eager, aggressive approach to nations trying to toss off their Soviet yoke could provoke a disastrous reaction by Soviet hard-liners — either tanks rolling into Eastern Europe or a coup removing Gorbachev from power — Bush made a point of measuring every response and statement.

"The world was fortunate to have his background and instincts at a turning point," said Robert Gates, who served as Bush's CIA director and deputy national security advisor. "The collapse and end of the Cold War look sort of preordained in hindsight, but for those who were there, it was not clear how it would happen."

Gates, who served in eight presidential administrations, suggested that Bush never received the credit he deserved for quietly "greasing the skids" that saw communists slide from power in the Soviet Union.

"He was a figure of enormous historical importance," Gates said. "There is no precedent in all of history for the collapse of a heavily armed empire without a major war."

Bush was sensitive to fears that some former Iron Curtain nations would rapidly move to align themselves with NATO. In conversations with Gorbachev, he assured the Russian leader that this was not the goal, and he sought to reorient NATO into less of a defense pact and more of a political association.

Bush understood that Gorbachev was under great pressure and feared that his position was increasingly tenuous. Ultimately, his fears were realized by a party revolt; Gorbachev survived to maintain leadership for a few months, then lost power as the old union dissolved. The first person he called when he was out of a job, just to say goodbye and offer thanks, was Bush.

"The way he avoided giving the hard-liners in the Kremlin any pretext to launch a coup was crucial," Gates said. "They finally did, but if they had launched it in 1989 instead of 1991, they might have been successful. Gorbachev's reforms would not have had time to weaken their hold on power. To underplay (American response) was the key. That kept the squeeze off Gorbachev."

The end of the Cold War did not mean an end to international trouble. When the Chinese government violently put down a growing dissident student movement, most notably in a 1989 confrontation at Tiananmen Square, Bush used his personal relationship with the premier to allay fears of American intrusion into Chinese matters. One of the few American figures trusted by Beijing, he was then able to dispatch a personal envoy to China to quietly discuss the issue.

Bush's careful conduct on the foreign stage was sometimes seen as timidity by critics. One such instance was a 1989 visit to Ukraine, then still a part of the soon-to-dissolve Soviet empire. In what quickly was dubbed by critics as his "chicken Kiev" speech, Bush warned against "suicidal nationalism." Freedom and political independence were different things, he said. Within months, Ukrainians voted overwhelmingly for independence.

In a return visit to Kiev in 2004, Bush said his remarks had been misunderstood and that he was only urging Ukrainians not to do "something stupid" that could have prompted a crackdown by Moscow. In later decades, his broader concern about nationalist impulses showed prescience, as the breakup of Yugoslavia led to war and genocide, and the movement of former Eastern bloc countries toward NATO brought increasing friction with Russia, and ultimately its support of an insurgency in Ukraine.

On his final foreign trip as president, Bush and Russian President Boris Yeltsin signed the second Strategic Arms Reduction Treaty during a glittering ceremony at the Kremlin at Moscow. The pact called for cutting their nations' nuclear arsenals by two-thirds over 10 years. Bush's bid for a "new world order" to replace the superpowers' rivalry was left undefined as his presidency ended.

The joy that marked the conclusion of the Cold War was replaced quickly by regional and ethnic, sometime even tribal, conflicts in Europe, Asia and Africa as well as terrorist tactics of radical Islamic

LEFT: Bush and Vice President Quayle confer with EPA Administrator William Reilly, Transportation Secretary Samuel Skinner and Admiral Paul Yost, Commandant of the U.S. Coast Guard, about the Exxon Valdez oil spill in Alaska a few days earlier in March 1989. Spread out on the floor is a coastal map of the area around Prince William Sound.
George Bush Presidential Library and Museum

fundamentalists. The biggest international crisis, however, was an old-fashioned ground assault reminiscent of another era.

In the summer of 1990, Iraqi dictator Saddam Hussein decided to end a simmering dispute over ownership of a large oil field by invading his small neighbor Kuwait and hover menacingly on the northern border of Saudi Arabia, which claims a quarter of the world's crude oil reserves and at the time was a major source of America's energy supply.

Bush quickly declared that the occupation would "not stand." With the grudging consent of Saudi leaders, he sent U.S. troops to the desert kingdom in what would become, to that point, the largest deployment of American military personnel since the Vietnam War. Bush also enlisted the support of many nations, including eight Arab countries, and waited for an international consensus before moving forward.

The ability of Bush to craft the Gulf coalition, with Baker's help, and prod the United Nations to fulfill one of its central purposes was a significant achievement. He skillfully managed to gain the support of China and Russia at the U.N. debate — Iraq had been a Soviet ally — and then coordinated a large joint military operation with longtime allies England and France. More than 40 nations contributed financially or in some way to the cause.

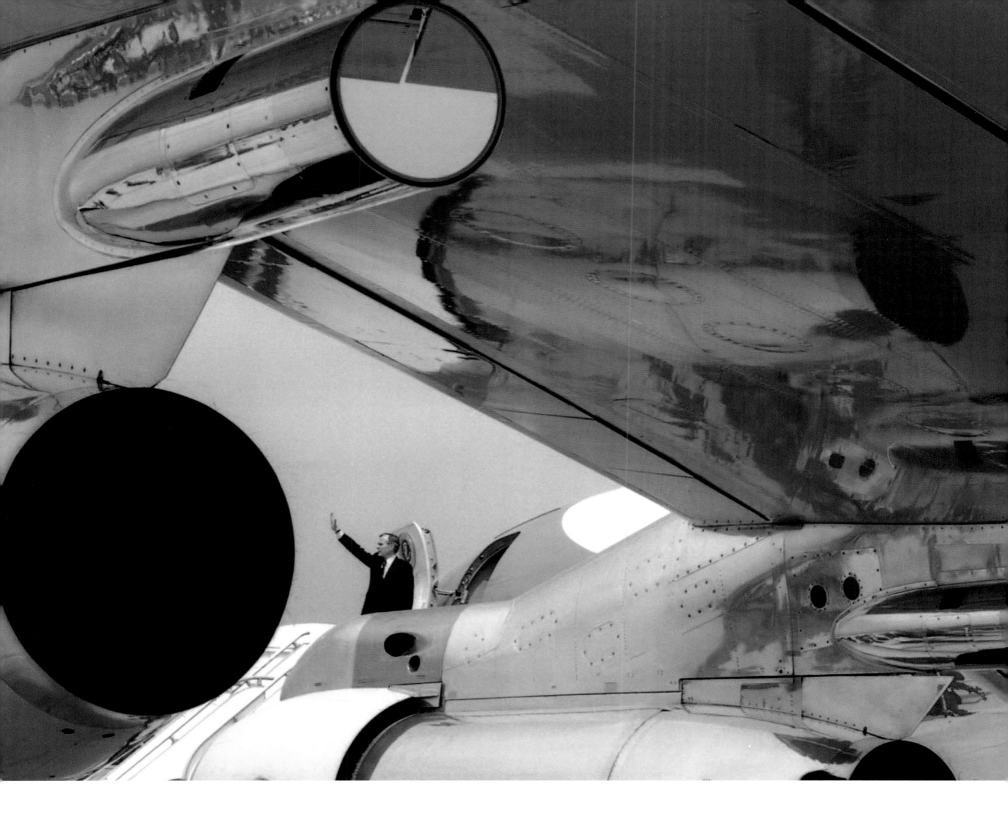

Bush had hoped economic sanctions and worldwide pressure would persuade Hussein, whom the U.S. had once assisted in its long war with Iran, to leave Kuwait. It did not. Force was the only option that had a chance of quick results.

A five-week air assault that began Jan. 17, 1991, was followed by a 100-hour ground offensive. Facing the full onslaught of Desert Storm, the Iraqi troops who were not killed quickly scattered or retreated northward. In one of the most controversial moves of his administration, Bush and his senior advisers decided not to send U.S. ground forces to pursue the fleeing units into Iraq itself, arguing that doing so would go beyond their U.N. mandate, fracture the coalition, and dangerously destabilize Iraq.

In his own hemisphere, Bush's presidential term saw negotiation of the North American Free Trade Agreement (eventually to be ratified in November 1993) and the U.S.-led coup to overthrow Noriega of Panama, who had been indicted in the United States on drug trafficking charges. Bush made the decision to take Noriega out of power following a series of small attacks on U.S. military personnel.

Following the Iraq war, Bush enjoyed enormous popularity, which led most pundits to assume a second term was all but assured. Bush knew better. Economic malaise was a fact of life that would outlive the war's patriotic surge, and he felt that increasing budget deficits were a drag that might see it spread. With Democrats in control of Congress, the only solution was a measure to increase government revenue.

Bush agreed to raise taxes. The reaction was brutal — "Read My Lips: I Lied," roared the New York Post — and his fellow Republicans were as harsh as anyone. The burgeoning ultra-conservatives led by Newt Gingrich claimed betrayal. They did not share Bush's view on "sound governance." They believed in ideological conformity and had no reservations about shutting the government down to get what they wanted.

ABOVE: Bush announces his selection of Gen. Colin Powell as Chairman of the Joint Chiefs of Staff, as Vice President Quayle looks on in August 1989. Powell would later serve in the administration of George W. Bush. *George Bush Presidential Library and Museum*

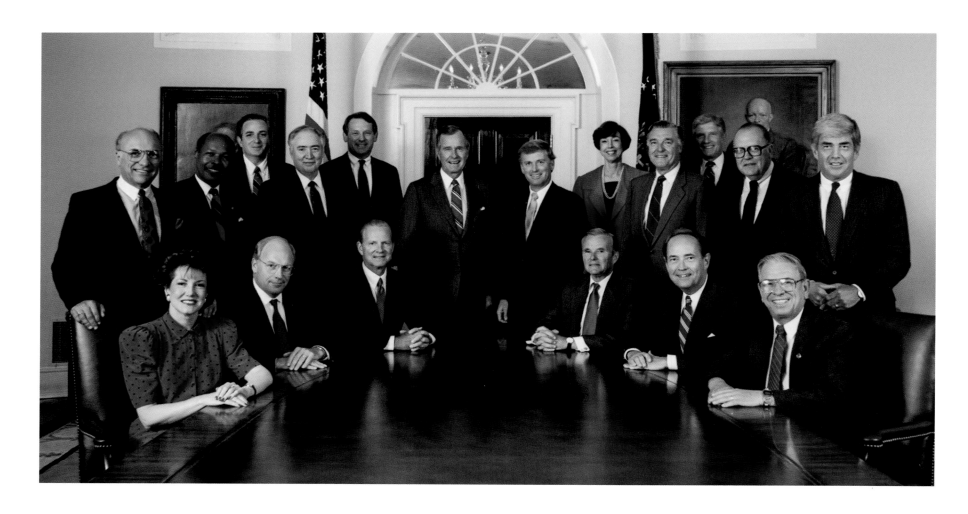

ABOVE: President Bush and Vice President Dan Quayle pose with cabinet secretaries for the official cabinet portrait in September 1989. Standing left to right are: Secs. Richard Cheney, Defense; Louis Sullivan, Health and Human Services; Richard Darman, Director of Office of Management and Budget; Lauro Cavazos, Education; Samuel Skinner, Transportation; Bush and Quayle; Carla Hills, U.S. Trade Representative; James Watkins, Energy; Robert Mosbacher, Commerce; Edward Derwinski, Veterans Affairs; Jack Kemp, Housing and Urban Development. Seated left to right are: Elizabeth Dole, Labor; Richard Cheney, Defense; James Baker, State; Nicholas Brady, Treasury; Richard Thornburgh, Attorney General; and Manuel Lujan, Interior.
George Bush Presidential Library and Museum

RIGHT: Few presidents have enjoyed sports and games more than Bush, so he was happy to show off the bowling alley at the Camp David retreat to Mexican President Carlos Salinas de Gortari during a visit in October 1989. *George Bush Presidential Library and Museum*

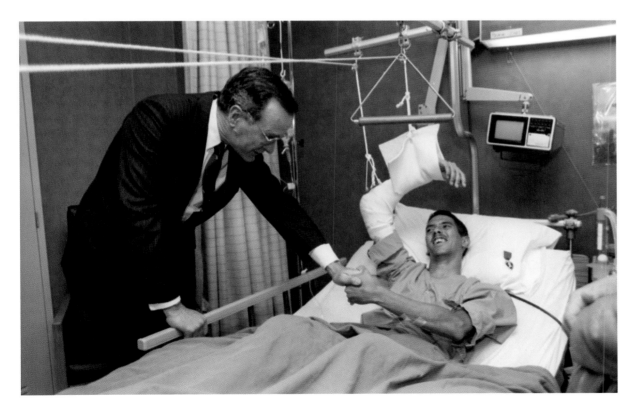

ABOVE: Bush shakes hands with young Acres Homes residents in Houston following a speech commending them for being part of an effort toward building a drug-free neighborhood. *Manuel M. Chavez / Houston Post*

ABOVE LEFT: Bush with Houston Mayor Kathy Whitmire following a speech at Andrew Winzer Park in which he commended residents of Acres Homes for their efforts to rid their neighborhood of drugs. *Manuel M. Chavez / Houston Post*

LEFT: Bush visits with a military service member at Wilford Hall Medical Center at Lackland AFB in San Antonio. The soldier was injured during Operation Just Cause, the 1989 invasion of Panama conducted in order to remove from power dictator and international drug trafficker Manuel Noriega. *George Bush Presidential Library and Museum*

TOP: Bush meets with five NASA astronauts who had recently carried out a mission aboard the Space Shuttle Columbia in January 1990.
George Bush Presidential Library and Museum

ABOVE: Bush blasts out of a bunker while playing golf with publisher Walter Annenberg near his home in Rancho Mirage, Calif., in March 1990.
George Bush Presidential Library and Museum

RIGHT: Bush acknowledges a gracious reception on Capitol Hill just before delivering his State of the Union message in January 1990.
George Bush Presidential Library and Museum

ABOVE: President Bush and German Prime Minister Helmut Kohl take a walk in the woods at Camp David on a cold February day in 1990. *George Bush Presidential Library and Museum*

RIGHT: Bush signs the Americans with Disabilities Act, one of his signature domestic achievements, in a ceremony in the Rose Garden of the White House in July 1990. Sharing the scene are Rev. Harold Wilkie, (rear, left), advocate for the disabled, Sandra Parrino of the National Council on Disability, Evan Kemp, (front, left), Chairman of the Equal Opportunity Commission, and Justin Dart, Presidential Commission on Employment of People with Disabilities.
George Bush Presidential Library and Museum

BELOW RIGHT: Bush talks on the telephone to President Ali Abdullah Saleh of Yemen regarding Iraq's invasion of Kuwait while in his suite at the Catto Ranch in Aspen, Colo., in August 1990.
George Bush Presidential Library and Museum

ABOVE: Participants at the G7 Economic Summit in Houston pause for a formal portrait at Rice University, July 1990. To President Bush's left are Jacques Dolors, President of the Commission of European Communities; Giulio Andreotti, Prime Minister of Italy; Helmut Kohl, Chancellor of the Federal Republic of Germany; and François Mitterrand, President of France. To his right are Margaret Thatcher, Prime Minister of Great Britain; Brian Mulroney, Prime Minister of Canada; and Toshiki Kaifu, Prime Minister of Japan. *George Bush Presidential Library and Museum*

RIGHT: President Bush participates in a full National Security Council meeting in the Cabinet Room regarding Iraq's military invasion of Kuwait.
George Bush Presidential Library and Museum

BELOW RIGHT: Bush walks with Saudi Foreign Minister Prince Saud al- Faisal, at Walker's Point during the busy summer of 1990.
George Bush Presidential Library and Museum

BELOW: Bush was among the first to learn that nowhere is safe from the intrusion of a cell phone call, as he has to pause during a round at Cape Arundel Golf Club to discuss matters involving Iraq. The clunky early portable phone is provided by aide Bruce Caughman.
George Bush Presidential Library and Museum

ABOVE: Ever on the phone, Bush speaks with Turkish President Turgut Ozal during a national security briefing with Defense Secretary Robert Gates and senior staffer Andy Card in the living room of his summer home in Kennebunkport, Maine, in August 1990. *George Bush Presidential Library and Museum*

RIGHT: An avid outdoorsman, Bush gets in a little fishing with daughter Doro during a visit to the family home in Kennebunkport, Maine, in September 1990. Goofy hats were always welcome. *George Bush Presidential Library and Museum*

BELOW RIGHT: Bush is accompanied by an uncertain granddaughter, Ellie LeBlond, as he walks down the driveway of the family's home at Walker's Point in Kennebunkport in August 1990. *George Bush Presidential Library and Museum*

BELOW: Bush enjoys a pleasant late-summer day as he does some work on the Colonnade of the White House. *George Bush Presidential Library and Museum*

LEFT: Bush and his son Marvin, wearing a Halloween mask, participate in a White House horseshoe tournament. The horseshoe pit was a constant venue for fun and relaxation during the Bush White House years. Even foreign leaders sometimes were invited. *George Bush Presidential Library and Museum*

BELOW LEFT: Bush dons a Stetson while talking on the phone at his desk aboard Air Force One in November 1990. *George Bush Presidential Library and Museum*

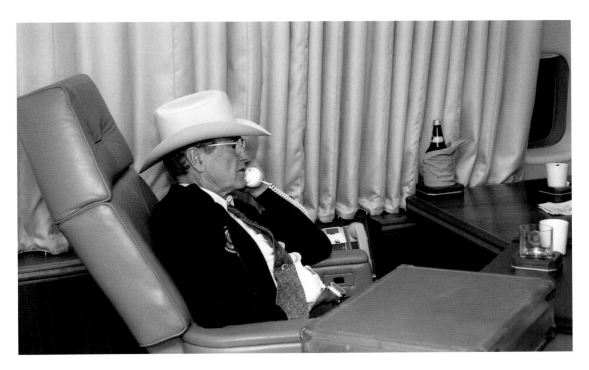

ABOVE: The First Lady enjoys conversation with troops of the 197th Infantry Brigade during a Thanksgiving visit that she and the president made to Saudi Arabia in November 1990.

George Bush Presidential Library and Museum

RIGHT: Bush sits in the cockpit of a fighter plane while visiting troops in Saudi Arabia.

George Bush Presidential Library and Museum

ABOVE: Bush rides in a Humvee with General "Stormin' Norman" Schwarzkopf in Saudi Arabia during the runup to the first Gulf War. *George Bush Presidential Library and Museum*

ABOVE: President Bush delivers the State of the Union address to Congress on Jan. 29, 1991. *George Bush Presidential Library and Museum*

ABOVE RIGHT: Bush along with senior staffers Robert Gates and Brent Scowcroft notify Congressional leadership of the bombing in Baghdad on Jan. 16, 1991. *George Bush Presidential Library and Museum*

RIGHT: Bush speaks in the Rose Garden of the White House in December 1990. He is accompanied by ambassadors from other nations involved in the coalition assembled as part of Operation Desert Shield. *George Bush Presidential Library and Museum*

LEFT: President Bush talks with his staff on Feb. 22, 1991, before announcing a 24-hour deadline for Iraq to withdraw from Kuwait in response to a Soviet peace proposal. *George Bush Presidential Library and Museum*

BELOW LEFT: General Colin Powell gives a briefing on the progress of the ground war with Iraq to President Bush and senior members of his staff in the residence office on Feb. 24, 1991.

George Bush Presidential Library and Museum

RIGHT: Bush announces to the nation the suspension of offensive combat operations in Iraq and the liberation of Kuwait, and lays out conditions for a permanent cease-fire in an address from the Oval Office on Feb. 27, 1991. *George Bush Presidential Library and Museum*

BELOW: Bush addresses a joint meeting of Congress to announce the successful conclusion of the military campaign to reverse the Iraqi takeover of Kuwait. *George Bush Presidential Library and Museum*

BOTTOM: In a May 1991 meeting following the Gulf War, President Bush is given a t-shirt by Prince Bandar bin Sultan, the Saudi Ambassador to the United States. The shirt shows Bandar in a tank saying "Hey Hussein."
George Bush Presidential Library and Museum

ABOVE: Bush meets with Secretary of Defense Dick Cheney, Gen. Norman Schwarzkopf, Vice President Dan Quayle and Gen. Colin Powell at the White House in April 1991.

George Bush Presidential Library and Museum

TOP: The Jogger in Chief takes a break to run with a group of people in Houston's Memorial Park in April 1991.
George Bush Presidential Library and Museum

ABOVE: Bush and comedian Bob Hope share a laugh in the Pool Garden at the Four Seasons Hotel in Newport Beach, Calif., in April 1991.
George Bush Presidential Library and Museum

RIGHT: President Bush plays a spirited doubles match with his son Jeb at the family compound at Walker's Point, Kennebunkport, Maine, in August 1991. Family competition often was serious business.
George Bush Presidential Library and Museum

LEFT: President Bush and Soviet Union President Mikhail Gorbachev take a walking tour of Kremlin Cathedral Square and Red Square on July 30, 1991. The two signed the Strategic Arms Reduction Treaty during the visit.
George Bush Presidential Library and Museum

BELOW LEFT: Bush delivers a televised national address from the Oval Office regarding developments in the dissolving USSR in December 1991, including the resignation of Gorbachev.
George Bush Presidential Library and Museum

BELOW RIGHT: Bush speaks by phone with Gorbachev in the bedroom of his home at Walker's Point, Kennebunkport, Maine, following a failed coup in the Soviet Union in August 1991. Bush expressed his personal support.
George Bush Presidential Library and Museum

RIGHT: All the then-living U.S. presidents gather for a photo at the dedication of the Ronald Reagan Presidential Library in Simi Valley, Calif., in November 1991. Pictured left to right are Presidents Bush, Reagan, Jimmy Carter, Gerald Ford and Richard Nixon. *George Bush Presidential Library and Museum*

BELOW RIGHT: Bush holds hands and sings "We Shall Overcome" with Coretta Scott King, right, and Louis Sullivan, a representative of the King Center in Atlanta, during a ceremony held for the signing of a proclamation to commemorate the Martin Luther King Jr. Federal Holiday held on Jan. 17, 1992. *George Bush Presidential Library and Museum*

BELOW: Bush kicks the ball in a Kemari exhibition in the courtyard of the Imperial Palace during a visit to Tokyo. Japanese participants are dressed in traditional costume. *George Bush Presidential Library and Museum*

ABOVE: Bush works the phone at his desk in the Oval Office in February 1992. He was constantly in touch with members of Congress as his administration worked to get proposed bills passed. His personal touch was widely known and respected, and he was close with members of both political parties. *George Bush Presidential Library and Museum*

RIGHT: President Bush plays
the piano for son George W.
Bush while waiting to greet
Anne Murray following her
performance at the Kennedy Center,
Washington, DC, April 7, 1992.
George Bush Presidential Library and Museum

FAR RIGHT: Borrowing a character
from TV talk show host Johnny
Carson, Bush portrays "Carnac
the Magnificent" during a skit
at the annual Gridiron Dinner
in March 1992. It had become a
custom for presidents to put in an
appearance at the dinner, which
is sponsored by the White House
Correspondents Association.
George Bush Presidential Library and Museum

BELOW RIGHT: Secretary of State
James Baker, left, and a White
House staff member talk on an
early form of cell phone while on
Baker's ranch in Wyoming in the
summer of 1992. Bush patiently
waits for his call to connect.
George Bush Presidential Library and Museum

LEFT: President Bush and Russian President Boris Yeltsin sign a series of military and economic agreements following a historic summit meeting in Washington in 1992. The two also negotiated a landmark strategic nuclear weapons treaty that significantly reduced the warheads in the arsenals of each nation. *George Bush Presidential Library and Museum*

BELOW LEFT: Bush signs the "Framework Convention on Climate Change Treaty" before his address at the United Nations Conference on Environment and Development in Rio de Janeiro, Brazil in June 1992. Critics claimed the treaty had been watered down to meet U.S. demands. It featured voluntary goals to reduce greenhouse gas emissions, not firm limits. *George Bush Presidential Library and Museum*

TOP: The president and First Lady pause for a quick family portrait with their son, George, wife Laura, and twin daughters Jenna and Barbara, during the Republican National Convention in Houston in August 1992. *George Bush Presidential Library and Museum*

ABOVE: A more comprehensive Bush family portrait from Aug. 19, 1992. Front row seated on the floor (left to right): Barbara Bush, Marshall Bush, Ashley Bush, Lauren Bush, Ellie LeBlond, Jebbie Bush. Second row seated: Laura Bush, Jenna Bush, Pierce Bush, Mrs. Barbara Bush, President Bush, Sam LeBlond, Jeb Bush, Columba Bush. Back row standing: Marvin Bush holding his son Walker Bush, Margaret Bush, George W. Bush, Sharon Bush, Neil Bush, Doro Bush Koch, Bobby Koch, George P. Bush and Noelle Bush. *George Bush Presidential Library and Museum*

RIGHT: Bush takes a moment during a respite at Camp David to pray for victims of Hurricane Andrew, which slammed into Florida on Aug. 23, 1992. The storm caused 44 deaths and about $25 billion in damage in the state. *George Bush Presidential Library and Museum*

ABOVE: Bush supporters pack the Illinois Farm Exposition during a campaign stop at the state fair in Springfield in August 1992. Despite their enthusiasm, the state and its 22 Electoral College votes were an easy win for opponent Bill Clinton. *George Bush Presidential Library and Museum*

ABOVE: President and Mrs. Bush give a symbolic nod to campaigns of yore with a whistlestop tour across Ohio aboard the train "Spirit of America" in September 1992. *George Bush Presidential Library and Museum*

OPPOSITE: Bush acknowledges one of his fans as his train pulls out of Bowling Green, Ohio. He narrowly lost the state in the general election. *George Bush Presidential Library and Museum*

ABOVE: President Bush stands with Canadian Prime Minister Brian Mulroney and Mexican President Carlos Salinas de Gortari in October 1992 at the Plaza Hotel in San Antonio, where they formally approved the NAFTA agreement. *George Bush Presidential Library and Museum*

ABOVE RIGHT: With the 1992 election almost at hand, Bush campaigns in Stratford, Conn., not far from the town where he grew up. *George Bush Presidential Library and Museum*

RIGHT: In one of the saddest moments of his political life, President Bush concedes the presidential election to Arkansas Gov. Bill Clinton at the Westin Galleria Hotel in Houston. Economic woes had eaten away at his early overwhelming popularity. *George Bush Presidential Library and Museum*

ABOVE: President Bush and Russian President Boris Yeltsin toast each other following the signing of the Strategic Arms Reduction Treaty in Vladimir Hall, the Kremlin, in early 1993.
George Bush Presidential Library and Musem

ABOVE LEFT: President Bush greets President-Elect Clinton outside the White House on Nov. 18, 1992. Although Bush was hurt and depressed by his defeat, his personality would not allow him to be anything but cordial and gracious toward his replacement in their first post-election meeting. In time, they became friends.
George Bush Presidential Library and Museum

LEFT: Following the election, the First Lady meets with Hillary Clinton for a traditional chat in the White House.
George Bush Presidential Library and Museum

Chapter Four

Citizen Bush

Conservative hero Reagan had gotten away with raising taxes and allowing budget deficits to float ever higher. To Bush was left the job of cleaning up a mess. He was intent on reducing the deficit, believing that doing so was needed to spark the economy. Because Democrats controlled Congress, he was caught in a squeeze. He could not reach a more balanced budget via spending cuts alone. Democratic leaders did not push him for a year, a conciliatory grace period. But eventually he had to agree to some measure to increase revenue. He said no to a hike in income taxes, but when Congress rejected the deal agreed upon by its leadership and the White House, personal tax rates had to be on the table.

Bush might have been able to finesse a few fee increases or small and less obvious tax hikes. This was more than that, and it hit him head on.

"It did destroy me," Bush later told biographer Meacham. "It was a mistake (to make the pledge), but I meant it at the time and I meant it all through my presidency. But when you're faced with the reality, the practical reality of shutting down government or dealing with a hostile Congress, you get something done."

Unlike politicians and presidents who followed him, Bush believed that a shutdown was tantamount to accepting defeat. Leadership sometimes meant making unpopular choices because the alternative was simply unacceptable. If you are not willing to make uncomfortable deals when you have to, what is the point of being in office?

Bush thought much had been gained through entitlement cuts and deficit reduction even if he had to give way on taxes. However, he did little to sell the benefits of the bargain to the American people. As

OPPOSITE: Bush joins his wife, Barbara and their grandchildren at the podium during the third night of the 1992 Republican National Convention in the Houston Astrodome.
Ira Strickstein / Houston Post

ABOVE: Bush thanks representatives from the Houston Police Department for their work during the 1992 Republican National Convention in Houston.

John Makely / Houston Post

ABOVE RIGHT: Bush speaks to supporters during his final campaign rally at Houston's Astro Arena on Nov. 2, 1992. Despite the enthusiasm of his hometown crowd, Bush knew that polls predicted defeat the next day.

Nuri Vallbona / Houston Post

many Bush observers have pointed out, he did not like making speeches or acting the part of salesman. Management was his responsibility, he felt. Do the best you can and move on. The thing will speak for itself.

As his reelection campaign came closer, it seemed apparent that Bush knew that the polls showing trouble were accurate. The crazy-busy first few years had taken a toll, and he was not sure he wanted to go through it anymore. Fatigued by the Gulf War and suffering from the early stages of Graves Disease, he talked often about not running again and going home to Houston. He was tired of the endless criticism and the backbiting in his own party.

Bush's spirits slowly changed as the innate competitive drive kicked in. Yet it was obvious that his candidacy lacked a theme or focus. He rejected suggestions that he announce something like a "Domestic Storm" (piggybacking on the Desert Storm military operation) as hokey. Long considered a blurry figure to the public, a candidate hard to pigeonhole, he seemed to have an identity problem despite his years on the national stage. He told those around him that he wanted another four years to tackle some of the domestic issues that had taken a back seat to the international turmoil, which he had handled with aplomb. But that was not a theme.

There was a noticeable pall over the campaign staff. Late in the campaign, Bush asked assembled political aides: "Am I the only SOB in the room who thinks I'm going to win?" That was just about the case.

Some insiders believed that Bush, knowing the Gulf War would be his historic touchstone, had not really wanted a second term. Some have contended he was, in part, talked into running again by senior advisers and friends who did not want to give Vice President Dan Quayle a clear shot at the Oval Office. Though it is likely that neither was correct, something wasn't quite right.

Marlin Fitzwater, Bush's press secretary, wrote in his memoirs: "The old zip was gone, and it was noticeable in the campaign. The old competitive juices that might have gotten the president into the 1992 campaign seemed to have lost their edge."

For all that, Bush still could not fathom the possibility of being defeated by Bill Clinton. He knew and liked Clinton, yet he also viewed him as a draft-evading womanizer little known outside of Arkansas. True, Bush had raised issues of trust by breaking his pledge on taxes. But he thought people should accept that he had done it because he had to, and for the right reasons. It was, he insisted, sound governance.

ABOVE: No longer president, Bush leaves Washington, DC, via helicopter in January 1993 to head to Andrews Air Force Base and a trip back home to Houston.

George Bush Presidential Library and Museum

Bush had spent the better part of two decades either dreaming of or competing to reach the White House. His last campaign could have been an opportunity to reconnect with voters, to somehow assure them the presidency was in the hands of an able captain, not a rookie with character issues. Yet it felt much more like an odious burden. His description was simpler. "All in all," he recorded in his diary one evening, "it's a pain in the ass."

The campaign became rowdy when allegations about Clinton's extramarital affairs became public, then

LEFT: The Bushes alight from Air Force One after the flight home to Houston following the inauguration of Bill Clinton in January 1993. The day marked the beginning of the next phase of their lives, when they no longer had to be concerned with the pursuit of high office. At last they were home to stay.

George Bush Presidential Library and Museum

turned bizarre when Ross Perot entered the race. Why the quirky Texas billionaire decided to mount an independent campaign was never clear. Bush was convinced much of it was personal, starting with Bush having declined a job offer in 1977. But whatever his motivation, Perot immediately shot up to the top of the polls as the plain-talking outsider who could fix a broken system.

Bush privately referred to Perot as "crazy" and a "strange little egomaniac" and wondered in his diary how voters could like someone "outrageously ill-suited to be president of the United States." Perot later dropped out of the race, then jumped back in at the end. When the election came, he managed to snare a whopping 19 percent of the popular vote, albeit zero in the electoral college.

Whether Perot cost Bush the election has been debated ever since. Bush believed it played a crucial role, but other analysts say many of the votes Perot commanded came from Clinton. The unarguable fact is that Bush was a one-term president, having failed to excite voters amid a slumbering economy.

In a diary entry, he called the 1992 campaign the "ugliest period of my life." Lifeless and out of sync, it never gained momentum. Then again, control of the White House typically moved back and forth

BELOW: Bush enjoys a moment with Houston Astros owner Drayton McLane in 1993, not long after McLane purchased the club. Bush, who had returned to Houston following his reelection defeat a year earlier, was often seen at Astros games sitting near home plate.
Kerwin Plevka / Houston Chronicle

between the two parties, and the GOP had held it for 12 years. The Cold War was over and Saddam Hussein had been turned back. As historians have argued, there was no overt reason for voters to embrace Bush and the status quo.

At a post-election dinner with Republican senators, Bush lamented his inability to "click" with the electorate. He acknowledged that his deeply held values of service, honor and decency, somehow must not have come across because of a generational gulf or his limitations with mass media.

"All the things I truly believe, they never came through — never ever," he said to Ann Simpson, wife of Sen. Alan Simpson. "And the media missed it, and the Clinton generation didn't understand it ... and I had not been able to communicate better what I really believe."

Fitzwater worked with him for years to improve communication skills and make him more comfortable in front of a camera, almost a requirement for modern politicians. It was tough sledding. One on one or in small groups, Bush was charming and expressed himself perfectly, Fitzwater said. The awkwardness began when cameras entered the room and the gathering took on a different character. His personality did not show through.

"It just wasn't there," Fitzwater said in an interview. "He had been taught so long by his parents and family about the artificiality of public relations and that sort of thing."

Over the years, Bush had been chided for a lack of apparent vision. Those who knew him understood it was not his nature to view himself as a visionary. Nor did he find it an essential trait. Some great presidents may have had great vision, but so do despots and demagogues. "What's wrong with trying to help people," he asked. "What's wrong with trying to bring peace? What's wrong with trying to make the world a little better?"

It had been only a few years earlier, as he stood on the precipice of obtaining the job he had so long

LEFT: Bush was a frequent speaker after leaving the White House. Here he attends a fundraiser in 2009, shortly after announcing he was gathering letters he had written and other material from his long career to publish a book. *Steve Campbell / Houston Chronicle*

ABOVE: Bush waves to friends as he arrives at the first Houston Hall of Fame Awards ceremony in 2000, which also celebrated the 30th anniversary of Bush Intercontinental Airport. *Steve Campbell / Houston Chronicle*

ABOVE RIGHT: It might look like a campaign whistle stop, but George and Barbara Bush are merely greeting well-wishers from the back of a train platform in Spring in November 1994. While she signs copies of her autobiography, her husband reverts to campaign mode. The couple were en route to College Station for the groundbreaking ceremony of the Bush presidential library. *Brett Coomer / Houston Chronicle*

coveted, that Bush had addressed Republican delegates to the 1988 national convention and offered his personal substitute for a statement of grand purpose — a promise of hope and moving forward, of a "kinder and gentler" nation, of a people illuminated by a thousand points of light. It was a moment that chafed at his innate tendency toward self-effacement, yet for a few minutes he was happy in the spotlight, telling his largest audience to date that he was the man to be entrusted with the presidential mission.

"And I will complete it," he said.

With the loss came intense pain, physical and emotional, that he fully acknowledged. Some of it arose from the frustration he felt by the end of the reelection campaign that the public did not understand him, and perhaps never had. Voters had heard the steady drumbeat of criticism, but they did not see the caring and empathetic person who lay underneath a sometimes awkward exterior, a man not given to public displays of emotion but who would cry easily in private, who always was eager to help the fellow who had less.

ABOVE: George and Barbara Bush watch a match at the U.S. Clay Court Championships in Houston in 2007. A good athlete and fierce competitor, Bush played tennis enthusiastically and often.
Steve Campbell / Houston Chronicle

ABOVE LEFT: Former presidents Bush and Clinton visit survivors of the tsunami that devastated much of Southeast Asia. The pair joined forces in 2005 to help raise funds for reconstruction. *Joe Reilly / USAID*

Democratic congressional leaders knew that Bush bore little resemblance to the cartoon figure of an aloof, out-of-touch, fumbling blueblood. Privately, some might have conceded he was the better person for the Oval Office in 1992. But politics was a world unlike others, and Bush had failed the ultimate test of selling himself.

Curiously, soon after the election, Bush's popularity began to surge, a belated acknowledgement that he had handled well most of what came his way. Former Speaker of the House Tip O'Neill stopped at the White House for a farewell chat and noted that in spite of having run a lousy campaign that he was "going out a beloved figure." Words of praise came from both home and abroad, in part because Bush had no real enemies.

"That's very nice," he confided to his diary, "but I didn't finish the job."

In his final personal thoughts about his time in the Oval Office, Bush wrote that he had tried to serve with honor, to do nothing that "would tarnish and hurt the presidency." He mused that no one seemed to care about that, especially the press, which was enamored with soaring rhetoric and great public displays of passion but uninterested in competent day-to-day performance as a more worthy quality.

"It does motivate me," he said of giving back through public service to a country that allowed his family to flourish. "But it's service with honor, service with a flair for decency and hopefully kindness ... serving without conflict, never for personal gain, always bearing in mind the respect for the office that I've been privileged to hold."

Coming back to Houston, Bush suffered a pervasive sadness, believing he had let people down by losing. There was much more to do that he feared would not get done. Convincing voters had been his responsibility, and he had failed. He did care, he did stand for something, he was engaged — this he

RIGHT: Bush's retirement brought a sudden and unexpected interest in parachuting, at least as a way of underscoring significant birthdays. He made his first jump as a young Navy pilot from a crippled aircraft. For his second, he waited until he was 75, another solo effort. Every five years brought another jump, albeit in tandem format as a concession to older bones. In this photo from 2009, Bush rides tandem with Sgt. Michael Elliott of the U.S. Army parachute team as he celebrates his 85th birthday in Kennebunkport, Maine. He has promised to do another when he turns 95.

SSG Joe Abeln / Army Golden Knights and George Bush Presidential Library and Museum

insisted was true, yet people did not want to believe him. That hurt more than anyone could know, he said.

Bush might have drifted out of sight into post-presidential retirement had it not been for his eldest child, George W. Bush, moving into the White House in 2000, only eight years after 41 had moved out. The Bushes were only the second father-son duo to reach the White House, almost two centuries after John Adams and John Quincy Adams served.

The father spoke infrequently to the press during George W's two terms and was especially circumspect about Bush 43's decision to invade Iraq and take out Saddam Hussein, an intervention that was based on the premise — faulty, as it turned out — that Iraq was pursuing weapons of mass destruction. The elder Bush was supportive but offered little unsolicited advice over the two terms. He made a point of keeping his distance, even in hindsight, though his biography in 2015 included a mild rebuke of some of his son's advisers.

Above all, Bush 41 understood that his opinions or judgments did not matter. As he later explained, he was no longer in the loop, lacking the sort of detailed information upon which to base a thoughtful decision, on Iraq or anything else. The last thing he wanted was to be seen by his son or his son's advisers as an unwelcome interloper. A nuisance.

LEFT: Bush stands in a golf cart to get a better view during the second round of the Shell Houston Open in 2007. Bush was an avid golfer who insisted on playing fast. *Brett Coomer / Houston Chronicle*

FAR LEFT: Houston Rockets center Dikembe Mutombo laughs as he talks with Bush before a game against the Timberwolves at Toyota Center in Houston, March 26, 2008. *Nick de la Torre / Houston Chronicle*

BELOW LEFT: St. Louis Cardinals first baseman Albert Pujols, left, and manager Tony La Russa introduce themselves to Bush before a game against the Astros at Minute Maid Park in April 2008. *Karen Warren / Houston Chronicle*

BELOW: Bush with Hannah McNair and Houston Texans owner Bob McNair before an AFC wild card playoff game at NRG Stadium, Jan. 7, 2017. *Brett Coomer / Houston Chronicle*

ABOVE: Bush is saluted as he arrives at the inaugural winter commencement convocation at Texas A&M University in December 2008. *Brett Coomer / Houston Chronicle*

RIGHT: Bush is serenaded by a Navy choir as he steps aboard the USS George H.W. Bush for a tour in 2009, in Norfolk, Va. *Smiley N. Pool / Houston Chronicle*

FAR RIGHT: Bush was overwhelmed by the Navy's 10th and last Nimitz-class supercarrier. It was a far cry from the USS San Jacinto, the light carrier that Bush served on during WWII that was close to half the Bush's length. *Smiley N. Pool / Houston Chronicle*

OPPOSITE: The aircraft carrier USS George H.W. Bush (CVN 77) while underway in the Atlantic Ocean. The vessel was conducting a joint training unit exercise. Bush considers having a namesake warship one of the greatest honors he has received. *Nicholas Hall / U. S. Navy*

And so he remained in the shadows, the off-stage remnant from a different era. Sometimes that was easier said than done, especially after the 9/11 attacks when America was expected to again offer global leadership. The elder Bush still carried within him a strong sense of duty and command. He had always been willing — perhaps eager — to shoulder the load of responsibility that had fallen on men of his class and generation.

"Once you've sat at that desk (in the Oval Office)," he confided to his biographer, "it's complicated to see someone else there. When you've made the big calls, it's tough to be on the sidelines — but you've got to be."

He had his own thoughts, for sure. Decades of experience in international diplomacy, government bureaucracy, and crisis management would have added up to decisions that could have been — likely would have been — significantly different than those taken by his son's administration. But it was not his place to suggest them unless asked. And most of the time he was not.

RIGHT: Bush sports a pair of American flag socks as he presents the newly announced Houston Texans cheerleaders with a rose during a ceremony announcing the new squad at the Texans training facility in 2013. As he began to make more appearances in a wheelchair, the socks became more prominent, and as a result, occasionally more outlandish. *Smiley N. Pool / Houston Chronicle*

BELOW RIGHT: Bush and James A. Baker, his longtime friend and former secretary of state, talk before the start of the 1st inning of a 2011 game between the Astros and the Cubs. *Michael Paulsen / Houston Chronicle*

BELOW: Runner Antonio Lopez-Perla shakes hands with Bush in front of St. Martin's Episcopal Church during the Chevron Houston Marathon in 2012. Bush's favorite spot was close to the 19th mile marker. *Mayra Beltran / Houston Chronicle*

Just as he was loath to offer opinions about his son's performance as president, Bush could not be persuaded to discuss even his own legacy of public service. His responsibility to posterity was to establish the George H.W. Bush Presidential Library at Texas A&M University, which contained all the archives from his administration. Looking back, evaluating things done or undone, calculating the effects or lack of them — it just didn't interest him.

"We don't like the L-word," Bush told the Houston Chronicle in a 2007 interview. "I think historians will get it right. The (presidential) library helps. There's material there for people to figure it out and get their own opinions of what we got right and what we got wrong. ... I'd rather not fool with it."

Whatever history's judgment, Bush was responsible for one achievement beyond dispute: The family name became synonymous with American politics. One son had used a stint as governor of Texas as a launching pad for the presidency. Another son, Jeb, served two terms as Florida's governor and later mounted his own campaign for the Republican presidential nomination. One of Jeb's sons, George Prescott Bush, was elected Texas land commissioner in 2014. Experts say his future looks bright.

LEFT: Bush throws out the ceremonial first pitch to Houston Astros starting pitcher Collin McHugh before the first inning of a game at Minute Maid Park in 2016. A lifelong baseball fan, Bush attended many games in the Astrodome and later at Minute Maid Park. *Karen Warren / Houston Chronicle*

Chapter Five

End of an Era

Having defeated Bush to win the White House, President Clinton went on to serve a second term. And when it was up, he remained on the political scene as his wife, Hillary, became a U.S. senator from New York. Every election cycle saw him campaign vigorously, give endless speeches, and raise money both for his wife and other Democratic candidates.

George H.W. Bush simply went home. Retirement meant disengagement, for the first time since his days in the oil business. Splitting time between his adopted Houston and his beloved Maine coast, he turned much of his attention to family, especially the younger Bush generations.

He did emerge for a different sort of campaign in 2004. He joined President Clinton to spearhead international fundraising efforts for victims of a tsunami that hit 14 Asian countries. The odd couple hit it off and became friends. The likable Southern chatterbox and the reticent and rumpled Yankee aristocrat reprised their charity work a year later for those displaced by Hurricane Katrina.

Retirement brought a more relaxed pace to a man who had always struggled with relaxation. So much of his life was spent looking toward the next task, facing the challenge still to be met. Now there were none, save for the periodic parachute jump. He decided to commemorate his 75th birthday with his first jump, a solo effort. He's done several more tandem jumps since,

OPPOSITE: Vice President Bush and his family, (from left to right), Doro, Marvin, Barbara, Jeb, George W., and Neil, host a post inaugural family reception at the vice presidential residence on the grounds of the U.S. Naval Observatory, Washington, DC, Jan. 20, 1981
George Bush Presidential Library and Museum

LEFT: George P. Bush gets a hug from his father Jeb, with his grandmother Barbara at the podium and his uncle Neil looking on, at the Republican National Convention in Houston, Aug. 28, 1992.
Dave Einsel / Houston Chronicle

RIGHT: Fireworks highlight part of the dedication ceremonies for the George Bush Presidential Library and Museum in College Station in 1997. As years passed, the library would play an increasingly important role in Bush's life. Primarily a research center, with over 44 million pages of archives and two million photos, the center also hosts numerous events and programs. Plans call for Bush and the former First Lady to be buried near the center grounds.

Smiley N. Pool / Houston Chronicle

the last when he turned 90.

As time went on, Bush's status as a beloved figure grew. Mostly unseen on the national stage, he was very much in view on the local one. TV cameras would catch him chatting with friends at Astros games, a fixture in his box near home plate at Minute Maid Park. The Texans remained another favorite, and he often was a guest in the suite of owner Bob McNair. Even when age and infirmity robbed him of mobility, Bush insisted on being wheeled onto the field to perform his role at the coin flip of the 2016 Super Bowl at NRG Stadium.

The Bushes also were regulars at the city's bigger charity events, reflecting a devotion to service work that had led the 41st president to establish the Points of Light Foundation in 1990 to encourage volunteerism and civic engagement. For their efforts over an extended period, the couple was honored in 2017 with the Mensch Award, bestowed by the Mensch International Foundation upon those who demonstrate commitment to tolerance and human rights.

"I want to speak as one of the proudest sons on the face of the earth," said Neil Bush, speaking on behalf of his parents at the award ceremony. "They are always reaching out and helping others, thinking of ways to make this a better world."

Neil Bush said his parents were especially disturbed over the 2017 attacks on Jewish cemeteries and community centers.

"My parents are here because we must speak out against the depravity in our midst and continue to condemn it in clear and simple ways," he said. This is "not a time for silence or ambivalence or indifference."

Long after much of the public had forgotten his four years in the White House, Bush remained dedicated to its remaining vestige, the presidential library, which was completed in 1997 and renovated

ABOVE: Texas Governor George W. Bush and Florida Governor Jeb Bush share a light moment with their father during a family photo session. *Steve Campbell / Houston Chronicle*

ABOVE MIDDLE: Barbara Bush offers her dog Bibi to GOP presidential candidate Mitt Romney during a visit to the Bushes home, Dec. 1, 2011. *Smiley N. Pool / Houston Chronicle*

ABOVE LEFT: Texas Gov. George W. Bush, right, answers media questions as his brother, Florida Governor-elect Jeb Bush, sits beside him. The brothers were attending the 1998 Republican Governors Association annual convention in New Orleans. *William Luther / San Antonio Express-News*

a decade later. He made a point of being there in December 2016 for the 75th anniversary of the Japanese attack on Pearl Harbor, just as he had been for numerous programs and award presentations. It is near the library and its 44 million pages of documents from his time in office that he and his wife will be buried. Little Robin Bush, forever 3, is already there.

There have been occasional moments in the national spotlight for the aging ex-president. In 2009, he was present for the commissioning of a new aircraft carrier, the USS George H.W. Bush. It was a thrill for the onetime naval pilot to behold the size and power of a ship that dwarfed the one upon which he had served, and to spend a night on board meeting the crew. Finding himself unable to sleep late, he took to wandering the halls and introducing himself to shocked sailors.

In 2010, President Barack Obama awarded Bush the Presidential Medal of Freedom, an honor that Bush himself had bestowed on Ronald Reagan. In the East Room of the White House, Obama spoke words that would have meant everything to Bush's parents and grandparents, who insisted that the advantages he enjoyed from birth were not to be squandered on self-indulgence or a life of no consequence. Success, achievement, praise — all had meaning only if they were earned.

"His life is a testament that public service is a noble calling," Obama said. "His humility and decency reflect the very best of the American spirit."

That as much as any accomplishment in any office could prove Bush's enduring legacy. He believed that no political party had a monopoly on wisdom, and that no aisle was too wide to walk across. Even in the heat of battle — with tempers short, language sharp and differences shouted — he could pick up a phone, call a political foe, and ask him to drop by for a drink.

As Bush's health has declined in recent years, slowly succumbing to the ravages of Parkinson's disease, so too has that of the body politic. The most genial of presidents has watched polarization that was beginning to cleave his party while he was president spread through a Congress all but incapable of compromising on significant issues. Many Republicans, especially those aligned with the Tea Party movement, took pride in announcing their unwillingness to work with a Democratic administration, in marked contrast to Bush's insistence that excessive partisan zeal was an impediment to good government.

ABOVE: Florida Gov. Jeb Bush laughs with his Texas counterpart, brother George W. Bush, at a campaign event in Austin in 2000 attended by 29 Republican governors. The rally kicked off a week of campaigning for Bush by fellow GOP statehouse leaders around the country.
Tom Reel / San Antonio Express-News

Yet even as the politics grew uglier with the coming of Donald Trump's administration, Bush refrained from public commentary. Time had passed, and he no longer felt a part of that world. By nature disinclined to retrospection, he rarely gave interviews and did not spend time evaluating the policies of subsequent administrations.

What he thought, in his waning days, of his own career is uncertain. To his biographer, he confided a lack of confidence that he never showed in his years of public service. He remarked at one point that historians might examine his presidency and find "an empty deck of cards."

Of such notions Obama, among others, was dismissive. He called Bush one of the country's most underrated presidents, insisting that his careful navigation through stormy waters kept the great powers away from confrontation and belligerence.

"I would argue that he helped usher in the post-Cold War era in a way that gave the world its best opportunity for stability and peace and openness," Obama said in an interview with biographer Meacham, whose retelling of Bush's life, "Destiny and Power", was published in 2015.

History may not cloak him in greatness, but Bush will be remembered as much more than the president who followed Ronald Reagan. He was the last world leader of a generation that restored order to a globe torn apart by madness. That should be enough.

LEFT: The father and son ex-presidents gather at midfield for the pre-game coin flip at a game between the Houston Texans and San Francisco 49ers in October 2009 at Reliant Stadium. Bush 41 has been a frequent attendee at Texans games over the years.
Brett Coomer / Houston Chronicle

ABOVE: Former President Bush laughs along with Barbara after a joke made by their son, President George W. Bush, during the commissioning ceremony for the USS George H.W. Bush aircraft carrier at the Naval Station Norfolk on Jan. 10, 2009. Capt. Kevin O'Flahery, commanding officer of the ship, sits between the former president and the president. *Smiley N. Pool / Houston Chronicle*

ABOVE: The two former presidents stand alongside Navy personnel before an NFL game between the Houston Texans and San Francisco 49ers at Reliant Stadium in October 2009. *Smiley N. Pool / Houston Chronicle*

ABOVE LEFT: Flanked by his father, President George W. Bush acknowledges the crowd during commissioning ceremonies for the USS George H.W. Bush just days before he left office. *Smiley N. Pool / Houston Chronicle*

LEFT: George W. Bush and his father walk onto the field before an NFL game between the Houston Texans and San Francisco 49ers at Reliant Stadium in October 2009. The older President Bush has been a fan of the team since it entered the league and is a frequent guest of owner Bob McNair. *Brett Coomer / Houston Chronicle*

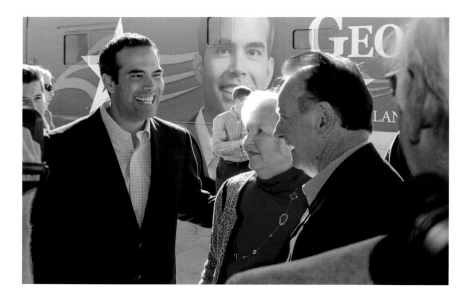

ABOVE: Jeb Bush spends a few minutes with his parents at a Salvation Army luncheon in Houston in 2013. Also pictured is Linda McReynolds, one of the organizers of the fundraiser. *Gary Fountain / Freelance*

ABOVE RIGHT: Texas land commissioner candidate George P. Bush speaks with former Republican Party Chairman Betsy Lake and Pasadena Mayor Johnny Isbell at the Southeast Harris County Republican Headquarters in Pasadena. The grandson of George H. W. Bush easily won his race for Land Commissioner in 2014. *Kirk Sides / Houston Community Newspapers*

RIGHT: A bust of George H.W. Bush is lifted on to a flatbed trailer along with other presidential busts created by Houston artist David Adickes. The busts were among the attractions of a residential development near Pearland. When the new subdivision faltered and faced foreclosure in 2010, the busts were removed by RWS Crane & Rigging employees and taken to a storage yard. *Nick de la Torre / Houston Chronicle*

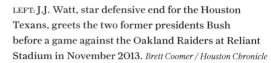

LEFT: J.J. Watt, star defensive end for the Houston Texans, greets the two former presidents Bush before a game against the Oakland Raiders at Reliant Stadium in November 2013. *Brett Coomer / Houston Chronicle*

BELOW LEFT: Texas Land Commissioner George P. Bush greets St. Representative Barbara Gervin-Hawkins after speaking at a rally for Texas Public Charter Schools on the steps of the Capitol in Austin in April 2017. He represents the third generation of the Bush family elected to public office. *Tom Reel / San Antonio Express-News*

ABOVE: Former first lady Barbara Bush claps and former president Bush salutes while watching the Memorial Day Parade in Kennebunkport, Maine, May 29, 2017.

Shawn Patrick Ouellette / Portland Press Herald